Promises
from
GOD'S WORD

Promises
from
GOD'S WORD

BakerBooks
a division of Baker Publishing Group
Grand Rapids, Michigan

© 2009 God's Word to the Nations

Published by Baker Books
a division of Baker Publishing Group
P.O. Box 6287, Grand Rapids, MI 49516-6287
www.bakerbooks.com

Printed in the United States of America

ISBN 978-0-8010-1338-6 (cloth)
ISBN 978-0-8010-7229-1 (pbk.)

A portion of the purchase price of this book has been provided to God's Word to the Nations. This mission society is being used by the Holy Spirit to promote and support a movement among God's people to be active participants in his mission "to seek and save people who are lost" (Luke 19:10).

Contents

God's Promises Help Me Know . . .

God Promises Help When I Feel . . .

God Promises That I Can Stand Against . . .

Through God's Promises I Experience . . .

God's Promises Enable My . . .

God's Promises Guide Me in . . .

Knowing God's Promises

God's Promises Offer . . .

Comfort

Blessed is the one who has concern for helpless
people.
The LORD will rescue him in times of trouble.
The LORD will protect him and keep him alive.
He will be blessed in the land.
Do not place him at the mercy of his
enemies.
The LORD will support him on his sickbed.
You will restore this person to health when
he is ill.

Psalm 41:1–3

Morning, noon, and night I complain and groan,
and he listens to my voice.

Psalm 55:17

My body and mind may waste away,
but God remains the foundation of my life
and my inheritance forever.

Psalm 73:26

This is my comfort in my misery:
Your promise gave me a new life.

Psalm 119:50

Let your mercy comfort me
as you promised.

Psalm 119:76

He is the healer of the brokenhearted.
He is the one who bandages their wounds.

Psalm 147:3

Even when you're old, I'll take care of you.
Even when your hair turns gray, I'll support
you.
I made you and will continue to care for you.
I'll support you and save you.

Isaiah 46:4

Sing with joy, you heavens!
Rejoice, you earth!
Break into shouts of joy, you mountains!
The LORD has comforted his people
and will have compassion on his humble
people.

Isaiah 49:13

Praise the God and Father of our Lord Jesus Christ! He is the Father who is compassionate and the God who gives comfort. He comforts us whenever we suffer. That is why whenever other people suffer, we are able to comfort them by using the same comfort we have received from God. Because Christ suffered so much for us, we can receive so much comfort from him.

2 Corinthians 1:3–5

If any of you are having trouble, pray. If you are happy, sing psalms. If you are sick, call for the church leaders. Have them pray for you and anoint you with olive oil in the name of the Lord. (Prayers offered in faith will save those who are sick, and the Lord will cure them.) If you have sinned, you will be forgiven. So admit your sins to each other, and pray for each other so that you will be healed.

James 5:13–16

Consolation

You have seen it; yes, you have taken note of trouble and grief
and placed them under your control.
The victim entrusts himself to you.
You alone have been the helper of orphans.

Psalm 10:14

Even though I walk through the dark valley of death,
because you are with me, I fear no harm.
Your rod and your staff give me courage.

Psalm 23:4

His anger lasts only a moment.
His favor lasts a lifetime.
Weeping may last for the night,
but there is a song of joy in the morning.

Psalm 30:5

The LORD is near to those whose hearts are
humble.
He saves those whose spirits are crushed.

Psalm 34:18

The people ransomed by the LORD will return.
They will come to Zion singing with joy.
Everlasting happiness will be on their heads
as a crown.
They will be glad and joyful.
They will have no sorrow or grief.

Isaiah 35:10

He certainly has taken upon himself our
suffering
and carried our sorrows,
but we thought that God had wounded
him,
beat him, and punished him.

Isaiah 53:4

Now you're in a painful situation. But I will see you
again. Then you will be happy, and no one will take
that happiness away from you.

John 16:22

Direction

Lovingly, you will lead the people you have saved.
Powerfully, you will guide them to your holy
    dwelling.

Exodus 15:13

The LORD is my inheritance and my cup.
    You are the one who determines my destiny.
    Your boundary lines mark out pleasant places
        for me.
Indeed, my inheritance is something beautiful.

Psalm 16:5–6

You make the path of life known to me.
    Complete joy is in your presence.
        Pleasures are by your side forever.

Psalm 16:11

God arms me with strength
    and makes my way perfect.

Psalm 18:32

The decisions of the LORD are true.
    They are completely fair.
    They are more desirable than gold, even the finest gold.
    They are sweeter than honey, even the drippings from a honeycomb.
        As your servant I am warned by them.
            There is a great reward in following them.

Psalm 19:9–11

Every path of the LORD is one of mercy and truth
    for those who cling to his promise and written instructions.

Psalm 25:10

A person's steps are directed by the LORD,
    and the LORD delights in his way.
When he falls, he will not be thrown down headfirst
    because the LORD holds on to his hand.

Psalm 37:23–24

Wait with hope for the LORD, and follow his path,
    and he will honor you by giving you the land.
        When wicked people are cut off, you will see it.

Psalm 37:34

Come, let's worship and bow down.
Let's kneel in front of the LORD, our maker,
because he is our God
and we are the people in his care,
the flock that he leads.

Psalm 95:6–7

Beautiful!

Gullible people kill themselves because of their
turning away.
Fools destroy themselves because of their
indifference.
But whoever listens to me will live without
worry
and will be free from the dread of disaster.

Proverbs 1:32–33

Trust the LORD with all your heart,
and do not rely on your own understanding.
In all your ways acknowledge him,
and he will make your paths smooth.

Proverbs 3:5–6

Arrogance comes,
then comes shame,
but wisdom remains with humble people.

Proverbs 11:2

If you give some of your own food to feed those
    who are hungry
    and to satisfy the needs of those who are
        humble,
then your light will rise in the dark,
    and your darkness will become as bright as the
        noonday sun.
The LORD will continually guide you
    and satisfy you even in sun-baked places.
He will strengthen your bones.
    You will become like a watered garden
        and like a spring whose water does not stop
        flowing.
Your people will rebuild the ancient ruins
    and restore the foundations of past
        generations.
You will be called the Rebuilder of Broken Walls
    and the Restorer of Streets Where People Live.

Isaiah 58:10–12

He will give light to those who live in the dark
    and in death's shadow.
He will guide us into the way of peace.

Luke 1:79

Encouragement

With you I can attack a line of soldiers.
With my God I can break through
    barricades.

Psalm 18:29

Some rely on chariots and others on horses,
    but we will boast in the name of the LORD our
        God.
    They will sink to their knees and fall,
        but we will rise and stand firm.

Psalm 20:7−8

Why are you discouraged, my soul?
Why are you so restless?
    Put your hope in God,
        because I will still praise him.
            He is my savior and my God.

Psalm 42:5

great scripture

God in his kindness gave each of us different gifts. If
your gift is speaking God's word, make sure what you

say agrees with the Christian faith. If your gift is serving, then devote yourself to serving. If it is teaching, devote yourself to teaching. If it is encouraging others, devote yourself to giving encouragement. If it is sharing, be generous. If it is leadership, lead enthusiastically. If it is helping people in need, help them cheerfully.

Romans 12:6–8

Everything written long ago was written to teach us so that we would have confidence through the endurance and encouragement which the Scriptures give us.

Romans 15:4

It was not God's intention that we experience his anger but that we obtain salvation through our Lord Jesus Christ. He died for us so that, whether we are awake in this life or asleep in death, we will live together with him. Therefore, encourage each other and strengthen one another as you are doing.

1 Thessalonians 5:9–11

God our Father loved us and by his kindness gave us everlasting encouragement and good hope. Together with our Lord Jesus Christ, may he encourage and strengthen you to do and say everything that is good.

2 Thessalonians 2:16–17

When people take oaths, they base their oaths on someone greater than themselves. Their oaths guarantee what they say and end all arguments. God wouldn't change his plan. He wanted to make this perfectly clear to those who would receive his promise, so he took an oath. God did this so that we would be encouraged. God cannot lie when he takes an oath or makes a promise. These two things can never be changed. Those of us who have taken refuge in him hold on to the confidence we have been given. We have this confidence as a sure and strong anchor for our lives. This confidence goes into the holy place behind the curtain where Jesus went before us on our behalf. He has become the chief priest forever in the way Melchizedek was a priest.

Hebrews 6:16–20

Forgiveness

a precious Scripture

If my people, who are called by my name,
  will humble themselves,
    pray, search for me, and turn from their evil
      ways,
then I will hear their prayer from heaven, forgive
    their sins,
  and heal their country.

2 Chronicles 7:14

The LORD protects the souls of his servants.
All who take refuge in him will never be
    condemned.

Psalm 34:22

Purify me from sin with hyssop, and I will be
    clean.
Wash me, and I will be whiter than snow.

Psalm 51:7

Various sins overwhelm me.
You are the one who forgives our rebellious acts.

Psalm 65:3

The LORD is compassionate, merciful, patient,
and always ready to forgive.

Psalm 103:8

O LORD, who would be able to stand
if you kept a record of sins?
But with you there is forgiveness
so that you can be feared.

Psalm 130:3–4

O Israel, put your hope in the LORD,
because with the LORD there is mercy
and with him there is unlimited forgiveness.
He will rescue Israel from all its sins.

Psalm 130:7–8

The LORD is merciful, compassionate, patient,
and always ready to forgive.

Psalm 145:8

"Come on now, let's discuss this!" says the LORD.
"Though your sins are bright red,
they will become as white as snow.
Though they are dark red,
they will become as white as wool."

Isaiah 1:18

I alone am the one who is going to wipe away
    your rebellious actions
for my own sake.
    I will not remember your sins anymore.

                  Isaiah 43:25

Let wicked people abandon their ways.
Let evil people abandon their thoughts.
Let them return to the LORD,
    and he will show compassion to them.
Let them return to our God,
    because he will freely forgive them.

                  Isaiah 55:7

The High and Lofty One lives forever, and his
    name is holy.
This is what he says:
    I live in a high and holy place.
        But I am with those who are crushed and
            humble.
            I will renew the spirit of those who are
                humble
                and the courage of those who are
                    crushed.
    I will not accuse you forever.
    I will not be angry with you forever.
        Otherwise, the spirits, the lives of those I've
            made,
        would grow faint in my presence.

                  Isaiah 57:15–16

I will pay attention to those
>who are humble and sorry for their sins
>>and who tremble at my word.

Isaiah 66:2

"But this is the promise that I will make to Israel after those days," declares the LORD: "I will put my teachings inside them, and I will write those teachings on their hearts. I will be their God, and they will be my people. No longer will each person teach his neighbors or his relatives by saying, 'Know the LORD.' All of them, from the least important to the most important, will know me," declares the LORD, "because I will forgive their wickedness and I will no longer hold their sins against them."

Jeremiah 31:33–34

Tear your hearts, not your clothes.
>Return to the LORD your God.
>>He is merciful and compassionate,
>>>patient, and always ready to forgive
>>>>and to change his plans about disaster.

Joel 2:13

Don't laugh at me, my enemies.
>Although I've fallen, I will get up.
>Although I sit in the dark, the LORD is my light.
I have sinned against the LORD.
>So I will endure his fury
>>until he takes up my cause and wins my case.

He will bring me into the light,
and I will see his victory.

Micah 7:8–9

Who is a God like you?
You forgive sin
and overlook the rebellion of your faithful
people.
You will not be angry forever,
because you would rather show mercy.
You will again have compassion on us.
You will overcome our wrongdoing.
You will throw all our sins into the deep sea.

Micah 7:18–19

While they were eating, Jesus took bread and blessed it. He broke the bread, gave it to his disciples, and said, "Take this, and eat it. This is my body." Then he took a cup and spoke a prayer of thanksgiving. He gave it to them and said, "Drink from it, all of you. This is my blood, the blood of the promise. It is poured out for many people so that sins are forgiven."

Matthew 26:26–28

Whenever you pray, forgive anything you have against anyone. Then your Father in heaven will forgive your failures.

Mark 11:25

Peter answered them, "All of you must turn to God and change the way you think and act, and each of you must be baptized in the name of Jesus Christ so that your sins will be forgiven. Then you will receive the Holy Spirit as a gift. This promise belongs to you and to your children and to everyone who is far away. It belongs to everyone who worships the Lord our God."

Acts 2:38–39

So those who are believers in Christ Jesus can no longer be condemned. The standards of the Spirit, who gives life through Christ Jesus, have set you free from the standards of sin and death.

Romans 8:1–2

Through the blood of his Son, we are set free from our sins. God forgives our failures because of his overflowing kindness. He poured out his kindness by giving us every kind of wisdom and insight when he revealed the mystery of his plan to us. He had decided to do this through Christ.

Ephesians 1:7–9

Get rid of your bitterness, hot tempers, anger, loud quarreling, cursing, and hatred. Be kind to each other, sympathetic, forgiving each other as God has forgiven you through Christ.

Ephesians 4:31–32

God has rescued us from the power of darkness and has brought us into the kingdom of his Son, whom he loves. His Son paid the price to free us, which means that our sins are forgiven.

Colossians 1:13−14

You were once dead because of your failures and your uncircumcised corrupt nature. But God made you alive with Christ when he forgave all our failures.

Colossians 2:13

Put up with each other, and forgive each other if anyone has a complaint. Forgive as the Lord forgave you.

Colossians 3:13

The Holy Spirit tells us the same thing: "This is the promise that I will make to them after those days, says the Lord: 'I will put my teachings in their hearts and write them in their minds.'" Then he adds, "I will no longer hold their sins and their disobedience against them." When sins are forgiven, there is no longer any need to sacrifice for sins.

Hebrews 10:15−18

If any of you are having trouble, pray. If you are happy, sing psalms. If you are sick, call for the church leaders. Have them pray for you and anoint you with olive oil in the name of the Lord. (Prayers offered in faith will save those who are sick, and the Lord will cure them.) If you have sinned, you will be forgiven. So admit your

29

sins to each other, and pray for each other so that you will be healed.

James 5:13–16

But if we live in the light in the same way that God is in the light, we have a relationship with each other. And the blood of his Son Jesus cleanses us from every sin.

1 John 1:7

God is faithful and reliable. If we confess our sins, he forgives them and cleanses us from everything we've done wrong.

1 John 1:9

I'm writing to you, dear children, because your sins are forgiven through Christ. I'm writing to you, fathers, because you know Christ who has existed from the beginning. I'm writing to you, young people, because you have won the victory over the evil one. I've written to you, children, because you know the Father. I've written to you, fathers, because you know Christ, who has existed from the beginning. I've written to you, young people, because you are strong and God's word lives in you. You have won the victory over the evil one.

1 John 2:12–14

Freedom

So if the Son sets you free, you will be absolutely free.

John 8:36

In the same way, brothers and sisters, you have died to the laws in Moses' Teachings through Christ's body. You belong to someone else, the one who was brought back to life. As a result, we can do what God wants.

Romans 7:4–5

However, the person who continues to study God's perfect teachings that make people free and who remains committed to them will be blessed. People like that don't merely listen and forget; they actually do what God's teachings say.

James 1:25

Growth

You are Peter, and I can guarantee that on this rock I will build my church. And the gates of hell will not overpower it. I will give you the keys of the kingdom of heaven. Whatever you imprison, God will imprison. And whatever you set free, God will set free.

Matthew 16:18–19

I am the vine. You are the branches. Those who live in me while I live in them will produce a lot of fruit. But you can't produce anything without me.

John 15:5

Don't become like the people of this world. Instead, change the way you think. Then you will always be able to determine what God really wants—what is good, pleasing, and perfect.

Romans 12:2

That is why you are no longer foreigners and outsiders but citizens together with God's people and members of God's family. You are built on the foundation of the apostles and prophets. Christ Jesus himself is the cornerstone. In him all the parts of the building fit together and grow into a holy temple in the Lord. Through him you, also, are being built in the Spirit together with others into a place where God lives.

Ephesians 2:19–22

He makes the whole body fit together and unites it through the support of every joint. As each and every part does its job, he makes the body grow so that it builds itself up in love.

Ephesians 4:16

Jesus Christ will fill your lives with everything that God's approval produces. Your lives will then bring glory and praise to God.

Philippians 1:11

All of God lives in Christ's body, and God has made you complete in Christ.

Colossians 2:9

Christ makes the whole body grow as God wants it to, through support and unity given by the joints and ligaments.

Colossians 2:19

Desire God's pure word as newborn babies desire milk. Then you will grow in your salvation. Certainly you have tasted that the Lord is good! You are coming to Christ, the living stone who was rejected by humans but was chosen as precious by God. You come to him as living stones, a spiritual house that is being built into a holy priesthood. So offer spiritual sacrifices that God accepts through Jesus Christ.

1 Peter 2:2–6

Healing

If my people, who are called by my name,
  will humble themselves,
    pray, search for me, and turn from their evil
      ways,
then I will hear their prayer from heaven, forgive
    their sins,
    and heal their country.

2 Chronicles 7:14

Blessed is the one who has concern for helpless
    people.
  The LORD will rescue him in times of trouble.
  The LORD will protect him and keep him alive.
    He will be blessed in the land.
      Do not place him at the mercy of his
        enemies.
  The LORD will support him on his sickbed.
    You will restore this person to health when
      he is ill.

Psalm 41:1–3

He is the healer of the brokenhearted.
He is the one who bandages their wounds.

Psalm 147:3

Let's return to the LORD.
    Even though he has torn us to pieces,
        he will heal us.
    Even though he has wounded us,
        he will bandage our wounds.
            After two days he will revive us.
                On the third day he will raise us
                    so that we may live in his presence.
Let's learn about the LORD.
Let's get to know the LORD.
    He will come to us as sure as the morning
        comes.
    He will come to us like the autumn rains and
        the spring rains
    that water the ground.

Hosea 6:1–3

If any of you are having trouble, pray. If you are happy, sing psalms. If you are sick, call for the church leaders. Have them pray for you and anoint you with olive oil in the name of the Lord. (Prayers offered in faith will save those who are sick, and the Lord will cure them.) If you have sinned, you will be forgiven. So admit your sins to each other, and pray for each other so that you will be healed.

James 5:13–16

Joy

You make the path of life known to me.
  Complete joy is in your presence.
    Pleasures are by your side forever.

Psalm 16:11

The Lord is my strength and my shield.
My heart trusted him, so I received help.
My heart is triumphant; I give thanks to him with
    my song.

Psalm 28:7

His anger lasts only a moment.
His favor lasts a lifetime.
  Weeping may last for the night,
    but there is a song of joy in the morning.

Psalm 30:5

We wait for the Lord.
  He is our help and our shield.
  In him our hearts find joy.
  In his holy name we trust.

Psalm 33:20–21

You crown the year with your goodness,
    and richness overflows wherever you are.
        The pastures in the desert overflow with
            richness.
        The hills are surrounded with joy.

Psalm 65:11–12

Let the nations be glad and sing joyfully
    because you judge everyone with justice
        and guide the nations on the earth.

Psalm 67:4

You make the path of life known to me.
    Complete joy is in your presence.
        Pleasures are by your side forever.

Psalm 116:11

Then our mouths were filled with laughter
    and our tongues with joyful songs.
Then the nations said,
    "The Lord has done spectacular things for
        them."

Psalm 126:2

Your dead will live.
Their corpses will rise.
Those who lie dead in the dust will wake up and
    shout for joy,

because your dew is a refreshing dew,
and the earth will revive the spirits of the
dead.

Isaiah 26:19

The people ransomed by the LORD will return.
They will come to Zion singing with joy.
Everlasting happiness will be on their heads
as a crown.
They will be glad and joyful.
They will have no sorrow or grief.

Isaiah 35:10

Sing with joy, you heavens!
Rejoice, you earth!
Break into shouts of joy, you mountains!
The LORD has comforted his people
and will have compassion on his humble
people.

Isaiah 49:13

Break out into shouts of joy, ruins of Jerusalem.
The LORD will comfort his people.
He will reclaim Jerusalem.
The LORD will show his holy power to all the
nations.
All the ends of the earth will see the salvation of
our God.

Isaiah 52:9–10

If you stop trampling on the day of worship
and doing as you please on my holy day,
if you call the day of worship a delight
and the LORD's holy day honorable,
if you honor it by not going your own way,
by not going out when you want, and by not
talking idly,
then you will find joy in the LORD.
I will make you ride on the heights of the earth.
I will feed you with the inheritance of your an-
cestor Jacob.
The LORD has spoken.

Isaiah 58:13–14

I will find joy in the LORD.
I will delight in my God.
He has dressed me in the clothes of salvation.
He has wrapped me in the robe of
righteousness
like a bridegroom with a priest's turban,
like a bride with her jewels.

Isaiah 61:10

I have loved you the same way the Father has loved me.
So live in my love. If you obey my commandments, you
will live in my love. I have obeyed my Father's commandments, and in that way I live in his love. I have told you
this so that you will be as joyful as I am, and your joy
will be complete. Love each other as I have loved you.

This is what I'm commanding you to do. The greatest love you can show is to give your life for your friends.

John 15:9–13

Always be joyful in the Lord! I'll say it again: Be joyful! Let everyone know how considerate you are. The Lord is near. Never worry about anything. But in every situation let God know what you need in prayers and requests while giving thanks. Then God's peace, which goes beyond anything we can imagine, will guard your thoughts and emotions through Christ Jesus.

Philippians 4:4–7

But be happy as you share Christ's sufferings. Then you will also be full of joy when he appears again in his glory. If you are insulted because of the name of Christ, you are blessed because the Spirit of glory—the Spirit of God—is resting on you.

1 Peter 4:13–14

The Word of life existed from the beginning. We have heard it. We have seen it. We observed and touched it. This life was revealed to us. We have seen it, and we testify about it. We are reporting to you about this eternal life that was in the presence of the Father and was revealed to us. This is the life we have seen and heard. We are reporting about it to you also so that you, too, can have a relationship with us. Our relationship is with the Father and with his Son Jesus Christ. We are writing this so that we can be completely filled with joy.

1 John 1:1–4

Justice

The Lord will not abandon [the righteous] to the
    wicked person's power
  or condemn him when he is brought to trial.

Psalm 37:33

Your throne, O God, is forever and ever.
The scepter in your kingdom is a scepter for
    justice.

Psalm 45:6

Let the nations be glad and sing joyfully
  because you judge everyone with justice
    and guide the nations on the earth.

Psalm 67:4

He brings about justice for those who are
    oppressed.
He gives food to those who are hungry.
The Lord sets prisoners free.

Psalm 146:7

He will gladly bear the fear of the LORD.
He will not judge by what his eyes see
 or decide by what his ears hear.
He will judge the poor justly.
He will make fair decisions for the humble people
 on earth.
He will strike the earth with a rod from his
 mouth.
He will kill the wicked with the breath from his
 lips.
 Justice will be the belt around his waist.
 Faithfulness will be the belt around his hips.

Isaiah 11:3–5

God showed that Christ is the throne of mercy where God's approval is given through faith in Christ's blood. In his patience God waited to deal with sins committed in the past. He waited so that he could display his approval at the present time. This shows that he is a God of justice, a God who approves of people who believe in Jesus.

Romans 3:25–26

Love

Lovingly, you will lead the people you have saved.
Powerfully, you will guide them to your holy
    dwelling.

                          Exodus 15:13

God loved the world this way: He gave his only Son so
that everyone who believes in him will not die but will
have eternal life.

                              John 3:16

I am in them, and you are in me. So they are completely
united. In this way the world knows that you have sent
me and that you have loved them in the same way you
have loved me.

                            John 17:23

We're not ashamed to have this confidence, because God's love has been poured into our hearts by the Holy Spirit, who has been given to us. . . . Christ died for us while we were still sinners. This demonstrates God's love for us.

Romans 5:5, 8

I am convinced that nothing can ever separate us from God's love which Christ Jesus our Lord shows us.

Romans 8:38

But God is rich in mercy because of his great love for us.

Ephesians 2:4

We understand what love is when we realize that Christ gave his life for us.

1 John 3:16

This is love: not that we have loved God, but that he loved us and sent his Son to be the payment for our sins.

1 John 4:10

Peace

The LORD will give power to his people.
The LORD will bless his people with peace.

Psalm 29:11

With his peace, he will rescue my soul
   from the war waged against me,
      because there are many soldiers fighting
         against me.

Psalm 55:18

O LORD, blessed is the person
   whom you discipline and instruct from your
      teachings.
   You give him peace and quiet from times of
      trouble
      while a pit is dug to trap wicked people.

Psalm 94:12–13

When a person's ways are pleasing to the LORD,
   he makes even his enemies to be at peace with
      him.

Proverbs 16:7

A child will be born for us.
  A son will be given to us.
    The government will rest on his shoulders.
    He will be named:
      Wonderful Counselor,
      Mighty God,
      Everlasting Father,
      Prince of Peace.
His government and peace will have unlimited
    growth.
  He will establish David's throne and kingdom.
  He will uphold it with justice and righ-
      teousness now and forever.
The Lord of Armies is determined to do this!

Isaiah 9:6–7

"The mountains may move, and the hills may
    shake,
  but my kindness will never depart from you.
  My promise of peace will never change,"
    says the Lord, who has compassion on
      you.

Isaiah 54:10

All your children will be taught by the Lord,
  and your children will have unlimited peace.

Isaiah 54:13

With perfect peace you will protect those whose
    minds cannot be changed,
  because they trust you.

Isaiah 56:3

I will promise them peace. This promise will last forever.
I will establish them, make them increase in number,
and put my holy place among them permanently. My
dwelling place will be with them. I will be their God,
and they will be my people.

Ezekiel 37:26–27

He will give light to those who live in the dark
    and in death's shadow.
He will guide us into the way of peace.

Luke 1:79

Now that we have God's approval by faith, we have peace
with God because of what our Lord Jesus Christ has
done. Through Christ we can approach God and stand
in his favor. So we brag because of our confidence that
we will receive glory from God.

Romans 5:1–2

Since Christ's blood has now given us God's approval,
we are even more certain that Christ will save us from
God's anger.

Romans 5:9

Protection

The LORD's beloved people will live securely with
    him.
    The LORD will shelter them all day long,
        since he, too, lives on the mountain slopes.

Deuteronomy 33:12

"Because oppressed people are robbed and needy
    people groan,
    I will now arise," says the LORD.
"I will provide safety for those who long for it."
The promises of the LORD are pure,
    like silver refined in a furnace.

Psalm 12:5–6

The LORD is my light and my salvation.
    Who is there to fear?
The LORD is my life's fortress.
    Who is there to be afraid of?

Psalm 27:1

Even though I walk through the dark valley of
    death,
    because you are with me, I fear no harm.
    Your rod and your staff give me courage.

Psalm 23:4

The righteous person has many troubles,
    but the Lord rescues him from all of them.
    The Lord guards all of his bones.
    Not one of them is broken.

Psalm 34:19–20

They will not be put to shame in trying times.
Even in times of famine they will be satisfied.

Psalm 37:19

A person's steps are directed by the Lord,
    and the Lord delights in his way.
When he falls, he will not be thrown down
    headfirst
    because the Lord holds on to his hand.
I have been young, and now I am old,
    but I have never seen a righteous person
    abandoned
    or his descendants begging for food.
    He is always generous and lends freely.
    His descendants are a blessing.

Psalm 37:23–26

The LORD loves justice,
and he will not abandon his godly ones.
They will be kept safe forever,
but the descendants of wicked people will be cut
off.

Psalm 37:28

Blessed is the one who has concern for helpless
people.
The LORD will rescue him in times of trouble.
The LORD will protect him and keep him alive.
He will be blessed in the land.
Do not place him at the mercy of his
enemies.
The LORD will support him on his sickbed.
You will restore this person to health when
he is ill.

Psalm 41:1–3

The LORD of Armies is with us.
The God of Jacob is our stronghold.

Psalm 46:7

Turn your burdens over to the LORD,
and he will take care of you.
He will never let the righteous person
stumble.

Psalm 55:22

You, O LORD, are my refuge!

You have made the Most High your home.
    No harm will come to you.
    No sickness will come near your house.
He will put his angels in charge of you
    to protect you in all your ways.
        They will carry you in their hands
            so that you never hit your foot against a
            rock.
        You will step on lions and cobras.
        You will trample young lions and snakes.
Because you love me, I will rescue you.
    I will protect you because you know my name.
When you call to me, I will answer you.
    I will be with you when you are in trouble.
    I will save you and honor you.
    I will satisfy you with a long life.
    I will show you how I will save you.

Psalm 91:9–16

If you fear the LORD, trust the LORD.
    He is your helper and your shield.

Psalm 115:11

The LORD protects foreigners.
The LORD gives relief to orphans and widows.
    But he keeps wicked people from reaching their
    goal.

Psalm 146:7–9

He is a shield for those who walk in integrity
in order to guard those on paths of justice
and to watch over the way of his godly ones.

Proverbs 2:7–8

The name of the LORD is a strong tower.
A righteous person runs to it and is safe.

Proverbs 18:10

Every word of God has proven to be true.
He is a shield to those who come to him for
protection.

Proverbs 30:5

Do not be afraid, because I have reclaimed you.
I have called you by name; you are mine.
When you go through the sea, I am with you.
When you go through rivers, they will not
sweep you away.
When you walk through fire, you will not be
burned,
and the flames will not harm you.

Isaiah 43:1–2

He promised to save us from our enemies
and from the power of all who hate us.

Luke 1:71

He promised to rescue us from our enemies'
power
so that we could serve him without fear
by being holy and honorable as long as we
live.

Luke 1:74–75

But the Lord is faithful and will strengthen you and
protect you against the evil one.

2 Thessalonians 3:3

Don't love money. Be happy with what you have because
God has said, "I will never abandon you or leave you."
So we can confidently say,

"The Lord is my helper.
I will not be afraid.
What can mortals do to me?"

Hebrews 13:5–6

We know that those who have been born from God don't
go on sinning. Rather, the Son of God protects them,
and the evil one can't harm them.

1 John 5:18

God can guard you so that you don't fall and so that you
can be full of joy as you stand in his glorious presence
without fault.

Jude 24

Provision

Certainly, goodness and mercy will stay close to
    me all the days of my life,
  and I will remain in the LORD's house for days
    without end.

Psalm 23:6

Fear the LORD, you holy people who belong to
    him.
  Those who fear him are never in need.
Young lions go hungry and may starve,
  but those who seek the LORD's help have all the
    good things they need.

Psalm 34:9–10

But I would feed Israel with the finest wheat
  and satisfy them with honey from a rock.

Psalm 81:16

The LORD will certainly give us what is good,
   and our land will produce crops.
Righteousness will go ahead of him
   and make a path for his steps.

Psalm 85:12–13

He provides food for those who fear him.
He always remembers his promise.

Psalm 111:5

He gives food to every living creature—
   because his mercy endures forever.

Psalm 136:25

The eyes of all creatures look to you,
   and you give them their food at the proper
      time.
You open your hand,
   and you satisfy the desire of every living
      thing.

Psalm 145:15–16

He fills the needs of those who fear him.
He hears their cries for help and saves them.

Psalm 145:19

Refreshment

The LORD is my shepherd.
    I am never in need.
        He makes me lie down in green pastures.
        He leads me beside peaceful waters.
        He renews my soul.
        He guides me along the paths of
            righteousness
          for the sake of his name.

                    Psalm 23:1–3

    They are refreshed with the rich foods in your
        house,
        and you make them drink from the river of
          your pleasure.
Indeed, the fountain of life is with you.
    In your light we see light.

                    Psalm 36:8–9

Oppressed people will see this and rejoice.
May the hearts of those who look to God for help
    be refreshed.
The LORD listens to needy people.
He does not despise his own who are in prison.

                    Psalm 69:32–33

Refuge

The eternal God is your shelter,
and his everlasting arms support you.
He will force your enemies out of your way
and tell you to destroy them.

Deuteronomy 33:27

The Lord is my light and my salvation.
Who is there to fear?
The Lord is my life's fortress.
Who is there to be afraid of?

Psalm 27:1

He hides me in his shelter when there is trouble.
He keeps me hidden in his tent.
He sets me high on a rock.

Psalm 27:5

Your kindness is so great!
  You reserve it for those who fear you.
    Adam's descendants watch
      as you show it to those who take refuge in
        you.
  You hide them in the secret place of your
    presence
  from those who scheme against them.
  You keep them in a shelter,
    safe from quarrelsome tongues.

Psalm 31:19–20

Taste and see that the LORD is good.
  Blessed is the person who takes refuge in him.

Psalm 34:8

The LORD protects the souls of his servants.
All who take refuge in him will never be
  condemned.

Psalm 34:22

Your mercy is so precious, O God,
  that Adam's descendants take refuge
    in the shadow of your wings.

Psalm 36:7

God is our refuge and strength,
  an ever-present help in times of trouble.

Psalm 46:1

Lead me to the rock that is high above me.
You have been my refuge,
a tower of strength against the enemy.
I would like to be a guest in your tent forever
and to take refuge under the protection of your
wings.

Psalm 61:2–4

Trust him at all times, you people.
Pour out your hearts in his presence.
God is our refuge.

Psalm 62:8

Whoever lives under the shelter of the Most High
will remain in the shadow of the Almighty.

Psalm 91:1

You, O Lord, are my refuge!

You have made the Most High your home.
No harm will come to you.
No sickness will come near your house.
He will put his angels in charge of you
to protect you in all your ways.
They will carry you in their hands
so that you never hit your foot against a
rock.
You will step on lions and cobras.
You will trample young lions and snakes.

Psalm 91:9–13

Even though I walk into the middle of trouble,
  you guard my life against the anger of my
    enemies.
You stretch out your hand,
  and your right hand saves me.

Psalm 138:7

The LORD is good.
He is a fortress in the day of trouble.
He knows those who seek shelter in him.

Nahum 1:7

Rescue

The Messenger of the LORD camps around those
who fear him,
and he rescues them.

Psalm 34:7

Righteous people cry out.
The LORD hears and rescues them from all their
troubles.

Psalm 34:17

The righteous person has many troubles,
but the LORD rescues him from all of them.
The LORD guards all of his bones.
Not one of them is broken.

Psalm 34:19–20

The victory for righteous people comes from the
LORD.
He is their fortress in times of trouble.

The LORD helps them and rescues them.
He rescues them from wicked people.
He saves them because they have taken refuge in
    him.

Psalm 37:39–40

I waited patiently for the LORD.
    He turned to me and heard my cry for help.
    He pulled me out of a horrible pit,
        out of the mud and clay.
    He set my feet on a rock
        and made my steps secure.
    He placed a new song in my mouth,
        a song of praise to our God.
        Many will see this and worship.
        They will trust the LORD.

Psalm 40:1–3

Blessed is the one who has concern for helpless
    people.
    The LORD will rescue him in times of trouble.
    The LORD will protect him and keep him alive.
    He will be blessed in the land.
        Do not place him at the mercy of his
            enemies.
    The LORD will support him on his sickbed.
        You will restore this person to health when
            he is ill.

Psalm 41:1–3

With his peace, he will rescue my soul
    from the war waged against me,
        because there are many soldiers fighting
           against me.

Psalm 55:18

Because you love me, I will rescue you.
    I will protect you because you know my name.
When you call to me, I will answer you.
    I will be with you when you are in trouble.
    I will save you and honor you.
    I will satisfy you with a long life.
    I will show you how I will save you.

Psalm 91:14–16

O Israel, put your hope in the LORD,
    because with the LORD there is mercy
        and with him there is unlimited forgiveness.
        He will rescue Israel from all its sins.

Psalm 130:7–8

This is what the Almighty LORD says: I will search for my sheep myself, and I will look after them. As a shepherd looks after his flock when he is with his scattered sheep, so I will look after my sheep. I will rescue them on a cloudy and gloomy day from every place where they have been scattered.

Ezekiel 34:11–12

Then I will repay you for the years
  that the mature locusts, the adult locusts,
    the grasshoppers, and the young locusts ate
      your crops.
      (They are the large army that I sent
        against you.)
You will have plenty to eat, and you will be full.
  You will praise the name of the LORD your
    God,
    who has performed miracles for you.
    My people will never be ashamed again.
You will know that I am in Israel.
  I am the LORD your God, and there is no other.
    My people will never be ashamed again.

                                        Joel 2:25–27

He promised to rescue us from our enemies'
    power
  so that we could serve him without fear
    by being holy and honorable as long as we
      live.

                                        Luke 1:74–75

I thank God that our Lord Jesus Christ rescues me! So I
am obedient to God's standards with my mind, but I am
obedient to sin's standards with my corrupt nature.

                                        Romans 7:25

There isn't any temptation that you have experienced which is unusual for humans. God, who faithfully keeps his promises, will not allow you to be tempted beyond your power to resist. But when you are tempted, he will also give you the ability to endure the temptation as your way of escape.

1 Corinthians 10:13

God has rescued us from the power of darkness and has brought us into the kingdom of his Son, whom he loves. His Son paid the price to free us, which means that our sins are forgiven.

Colossians 1:13–14

From you the Lord's word has spread out not only through the province of Macedonia and Greece but also to people everywhere who have heard about your faith in God. We don't need to say a thing about it. They talk about how you welcomed us when we arrived. They even report how you turned away from false gods to serve the real, living God and to wait for his Son to come from heaven. His Son is Jesus, whom he brought back to life. Jesus is the one who rescues us from God's coming anger.

1 Thessalonians 1:8–10

Since the Lord did all this, he knows how to rescue godly people when they are tested. He also knows how to hold immoral people for punishment on the day of judgment.

2 Peter 2:9

People can know our Lord and Savior Jesus Christ and escape the world's filth.

2 Peter 2:20

Rest

I look up toward the mountains.
  Where can I find help?
My help comes from the LORD,
  the maker of heaven and earth.
He will not let you fall.
  Your guardian will not fall asleep.
Indeed, the Guardian of Israel never rests or
    sleeps.
The LORD is your guardian.
The LORD is the shade over your right hand.
  The sun will not beat down on you during the
      day,
    nor will the moon at night.
The LORD guards you from every evil.
  He guards your life.
The LORD guards you as you come and go,
  now and forever.

Psalm 121

Come to me, all who are tired from carrying heavy loads, and I will give you rest. Place my yoke over your shoulders, and learn from me, because I am gentle and humble. Then you will find rest for yourselves because my yoke is easy and my burden is light.

Matthew 11:28–30

Jesus answered her, "Everyone who drinks this water will become thirsty again. But those who drink the water that I will give them will never become thirsty again. In fact, the water I will give them will become in them a spring that gushes up to eternal life."

John 4:13

God's promise that we may enter his place of rest still stands. We are afraid that some of you think you won't enter his place of rest.

Hebrews 4:1

We who believe are entering that place of rest.

Hebrews 4:3

Therefore, a time of rest and worship exists for God's people. Those who entered his place of rest also rested from their work as God did from his.

Hebrews 4:9–10

Restoration

If only salvation for Israel would come from
   Zion!
When God restores the fortunes of his people,
   Jacob will rejoice.
   Israel will be glad.

Psalm 53:6

You have made me endure many terrible
   troubles.
You restore me to life again.
You bring me back from the depths of the
   earth.

Psalm 71:20

Don't you know?
   Haven't you heard?
The eternal God, the LORD, the Creator of the
   ends of the earth,
   doesn't grow tired or become weary.
      His understanding is beyond reach.
He gives strength to those who grow tired

and increases the strength of those who are
weak.
Even young people grow tired and become weary,
and young men will stumble and fall.
Yet, the strength of those who wait with hope in
the LORD
will be renewed.
They will soar on wings like eagles.
They will run and won't become weary.
They will walk and won't grow tired.

Isaiah 40:28–31

This is what the LORD says:
In the time of favor I will answer you.
In the day of salvation I will help you.
I will protect you.
I will appoint you as my promise to the people.
You will restore the land.
You will make them inherit the desolate
inheritance.

Isaiah 49:8

Security

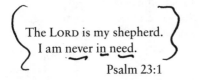

The LORD is my shepherd.
I am never in need.
Psalm 23:1

Yet, the LORD is enthroned forever.
   He has set up his throne for judgment.
   He alone judges the world with righteousness.
   He judges its people fairly.
The LORD is a stronghold for the oppressed,
   a stronghold in times of trouble.
Those who know your name trust you, O LORD,
   because you have never deserted those who seek
       your help.

Psalm 9:7–10

Strength

Lovingly, you will lead the people you have saved.
Powerfully, you will guide them to your holy
    dwelling.

Exodus 15:13

God arms me with strength
  and makes my way perfect.

Psalm 18:32

The LORD is my strength and my shield.
My heart trusted him, so I received help.
My heart is triumphant; I give thanks to him with
    my song.
The LORD is the strength of his people
  and a fortress for the victory of his Messiah.

Psalm 28:7–8

The LORD will give power to his people.
The LORD will bless his people with peace.

Psalm 29:11

With you we can walk over our enemies.
With your name we can trample those who
    attack us.

Psalm 44:5

God is our refuge and strength,
    an ever-present help in times of trouble.

Psalm 46:1

The things we had only heard about, we have now
    seen
    in the city of the Lord of Armies,
    in the city of our God.
        God makes Zion stand firm forever.

Psalm 48:8

O my strength, I watch for you!
    God is my stronghold, my merciful God!
God will come to meet me.
He will let me gloat over those who spy on me.

Psalm 59:9–10

With God we will display great strength.
    He will trample our enemies.

Psalm 60:12

Lead me to the rock that is high above me.
    You have been my refuge,
        a tower of strength against the enemy.

I would like to be a guest in your tent forever
and to take refuge under the protection of your
wings.

Psalm 61:2–4

God, the God of Israel, is awe-inspiring in his
holy place.
He gives strength and power to his people.
Thanks be to God!

Psalm 68:35

The name of the LORD is a strong tower.
A righteous person runs to it and is safe.

Proverbs 18:10

Look! God is my Savior.
I am confident and unafraid,
because the LORD is my strength and my song.
He is my Savior.

Isaiah 12:2

He gives strength to those who grow tired
and increases the strength of those who are
weak.
Even young people grow tired and become weary,
and young men will stumble and fall.
Yet, the strength of those who wait with hope in
the LORD

will be renewed.
They will soar on wings like eagles.
They will run and won't become weary.
They will walk and won't grow tired.

Isaiah 40:29–31

Don't be afraid, because I am with you.
Don't be intimidated; I am your God.
I will strengthen you.

Isaiah 41:10

The LORD will continually guide you
and satisfy you even in sun-baked places.
He will strengthen your bones.
You will become like a watered garden
and like a spring whose water does not stop
flowing.

Isaiah 58:11

The LORD Almighty is my strength.
He makes my feet like those of a deer.
He makes me walk on the mountains.

Habakkuk 3:19

God can strengthen you by the Good News and the message I tell about Jesus Christ. He can strengthen you by revealing the mystery that was kept in silence for a very long time but now is publicly known.

Romans 16:25–26

He will continue to give you strength until the end so that no one can accuse you of anything on the day of our Lord Jesus Christ. God faithfully keeps his promises. He called you to be partners with his Son Jesus Christ our Lord.

1 Corinthians 1:8–9

The weapons we use in our fight are not made by humans. Rather, they are powerful weapons from God. With them we destroy people's defenses, that is, their arguments and all their intellectual arrogance that oppose the knowledge of God. We take every thought captive so that it is obedient to Christ.

2 Corinthians 10:4–5

Therefore, to keep me from becoming conceited, I am forced to deal with a recurring problem. That problem, Satan's messenger, torments me to keep me from being conceited. I begged the Lord three times to take it away from me. But he told me: "My kindness is all you need. My power is strongest when you are weak." So I will brag even more about my weaknesses in order that Christ's power will live in me. Therefore, I accept weakness, mistreatment, hardship, persecution, and difficulties suffered for Christ. It's clear that when I'm weak, I'm strong.

2 Corinthians 12:7–10

I'm asking God to give you a gift from the wealth of his glory. I pray that he would give you inner strength and power through his Spirit.

Ephesians 3:16

Finally, receive your power from the Lord and from his mighty strength. Put on all the armor that God supplies. In this way you can take a stand against the devil's strategies. This is not a wrestling match against a human opponent. We are wrestling with rulers, authorities, the powers who govern this world of darkness, and spiritual forces that control evil in the heavenly world. For this reason, take up all the armor that God supplies. Then you will be able to take a stand during these evil days. Once you have overcome all obstacles, you will be able to stand your ground.

Ephesians 6:10–13

I can do everything through Christ who strengthens me.

Philippians 4:13

We also pray that the Lord will greatly increase your love for each other and for everyone else, just as we love you. Then he will strengthen you to be holy. Then you will be blameless in the presence of our God and Father when our Lord Jesus comes with all God's holy people.

1 Thessalonians 3:12–13

But the Lord is faithful and will strengthen you and protect you against the evil one.

2 Thessalonians 3:3

God didn't give us a cowardly spirit but a spirit of power, love, and good judgment.

2 Timothy 1:7

My child, find your source of strength in the kindness of Christ Jesus.

2 Timothy 2:1

Success

Never stop reciting these teachings. You must think about them night and day so that you will faithfully do everything written in them. Only then will you prosper and succeed.

Joshua 1:8

How can a young person keep his life pure?
    He can do it by holding on to your word.
I wholeheartedly searched for you.
    Do not let me wander away from your
        commandments.
I have treasured your promise in my heart
    so that I may not sin against you.

Psalm 119:9–11

Do not let mercy and truth leave you.
Fasten them around your neck.
Write them on the tablet of your heart.
    Then you will find favor and much success
        in the sight of God and humanity.
Trust the LORD with all your heart,
    and do not rely on your own understanding.

In all your ways acknowledge him,
   and he will make your paths smooth.

                    Proverbs 3:3–6

Entrust your efforts to the LORD,
   and your plans will succeed.

                    Proverbs 16:3

Whoever gives attention to the LORD's word
      prospers,
   and blessed is the person who trusts the LORD.

                    Proverbs 16:20

On the heels of humility (the fear of the LORD)
   are riches and honor and life.

                    Proverbs 22:4

Then he replied, "This is the word the LORD spoke to
Zerubbabel: You won't succeed by might or by power,
but by my Spirit, says the LORD of Armies."

                    Zechariah 4:6

Victory

The eternal God is your shelter,
    and his everlasting arms support you.
He will force your enemies out of your way
    and tell you to destroy them.

Deuteronomy 33:27

With you I can attack a line of soldiers.
With my God I can break through
    barricades.

Psalm 18:29

Some rely on chariots and others on horses,
    but we will boast in the name of the LORD our
        God.
    They will sink to their knees and fall,
        but we will rise and stand firm.

Psalm 20:7–8

No one who waits for you will ever be put to
    shame,
    but all who are unfaithful will be put to shame.

Psalm 25:3

The LORD is my strength and my shield.
My heart trusted him, so I received help.
My heart is triumphant; I give thanks to him with
my song.

Psalm 28:7

Then my enemies will retreat when I call to you.
This I know: God is on my side.

Psalm 56:9

Trust him at all times, you people.
Pour out your hearts in his presence.
God is our refuge.

Psalm 62:8

The God who is in his holy dwelling place
is the father of the fatherless and the defender
of widows.
God places lonely people in families.
He leads prisoners out of prison into produc-
tive lives,
but rebellious people must live in an unpro-
ductive land.

Psalm 68:5–6

The LORD supports everyone who falls.
He straightens the backs of those who are bent
over.

Psalm 145:14

Do not be afraid of sudden terror
or of the destruction of wicked people when it
comes.
The Lord will be your confidence.
He will keep your foot from getting caught.

Proverbs 3:25–26

He gives strength to those who grow tired
and increases the strength of those who are weak.
Even young people grow tired and become weary,
and young men will stumble and fall.
Yet, the strength of those who wait with hope in
the Lord
will be renewed.
They will soar on wings like eagles.
They will run and won't become weary.
They will walk and won't grow tired.

Isaiah 40:29–31

Don't be afraid, because I am with you.
Don't be intimidated; I am your God.
I will strengthen you.

Isaiah 41:10

Even when you're old, I'll take care of you.
Even when your hair turns gray, I'll support
you.
I made you and will continue to care for you.
I'll support you and save you.

Isaiah 46:4

Blessed is the person who trusts the LORD.
The LORD will be his confidence.

Jeremiah 17:7

But that's not all. We also brag when we are suffering. We know that suffering creates endurance, endurance creates character, and character creates confidence. We're not ashamed to have this confidence, because God's love has been poured into our hearts by the Holy Spirit, who has been given to us.

Romans 5:3–5

We know that all things work together for the good of those who love God—those whom he has called according to his plan.

Romans 8:28

Everything written long ago was written to teach us so that we would have confidence through the endurance and encouragement which the Scriptures give us.

Romans 15:4

When this body that decays is changed into a body that cannot decay, and this mortal body is changed into a body that will live forever, then the teaching of Scripture will come true:

"Death is turned into victory!
Death, where is your victory?
Death, where is your sting?"

Sin gives death its sting, and God's standards give sin its power. Thank God that he gives us the victory through our Lord Jesus Christ.

1 Corinthians 15:54–57

Christ gives us confidence about you in God's presence. By ourselves we are not qualified in any way to claim that we can do anything. Rather, God makes us qualified. He has also qualified us to be ministers of a new promise, a spiritual promise, not a written one. Clearly, what was written brings death, but the Spirit brings life.

2 Corinthians 3:4–6

I'm convinced that God, who began this good work in you, will carry it through to completion on the day of Christ Jesus.

Philippians 1:6

Faith knows the power that his coming back to life gives and what it means to share his suffering. In this way I'm becoming like him in his death, with the confidence that I'll come back to life from the dead.

Philippians 3:10–11

We need to hold on to our declaration of faith: We have a superior chief priest who has gone through the heavens. That person is Jesus, the Son of God. We have a chief priest who is able to sympathize with our weaknesses. He was tempted in every way that we are, but he didn't sin. So we can go confidently to the throne of God's kindness to receive mercy and find kindness, which will help us at the right time.

Hebrews 4:14–16

We want each of you to prove that you're working hard so that you will remain confident until the end. Then, instead of being lazy, you will imitate those who are receiving the promises through faith and patience.

Hebrews 6:11–12

When people take oaths, they base their oaths on someone greater than themselves. Their oaths guarantee what they say and end all arguments. God wouldn't change his plan. He wanted to make this perfectly clear to those who would receive his promise, so he took an oath. God did this so that we would be encouraged. God cannot lie when he takes an oath or makes a promise. These two things can never be changed. Those of us who have taken refuge in him hold on to the confidence we have been given. We have this confidence as a sure and strong anchor for our lives. This confidence goes into the holy place behind the curtain where Jesus went before us on our behalf. He has become the chief priest forever in the way Melchizedek was a priest.

Hebrews 6:16–20

Now, dear children, live in Christ. Then, when he appears we will have confidence, and when he comes we won't turn from him in shame. If you know that Christ has God's approval, you also know that everyone who does what God approves of has been born from God.

1 John 2:28–29

This is how we will know that we belong to the truth and how we will be reassured in his presence. Whenever our conscience condemns us, we will be reassured that God is greater than our conscience and knows everything.

1 John 3:19–20

No fear exists where his love is. Rather, perfect love gets rid of fear, because fear involves punishment. The person who lives in fear doesn't have perfect love.

1 John 4:18

Don't be afraid of what you are going to suffer. The devil is going to throw some of you into prison so that you may be tested. Your suffering will go on for ten days. Be faithful until death, and I will give you the crown of life.

Revelation 2:10

God's Promises Help
Me Know . . .

The Future

Lovingly, you will lead the people you have saved.
Powerfully, you will guide them to your holy
    dwelling.

Exodus 15:13

Certainly, goodness and mercy will stay close to
    me all the days of my life,
and I will remain in the LORD's house for days
    without end.

Psalm 23:6

We wait for the LORD.
    He is our help and our shield.
    In him our hearts find joy.
    In his holy name we trust.

Psalm 33:20–21

Wait with hope for the LORD, and follow his path,
    and he will honor you by giving you the land.
    When wicked people are cut off, you will see
    it.

Psalm 37:34

With his peace, he will rescue my soul
    from the war waged against me,
        because there are many soldiers fighting
            against me.

Psalm 55:18

Because you love me, I will rescue you.
    I will protect you because you know my name.
When you call to me, I will answer you.
    I will be with you when you are in trouble.
    I will save you and honor you.
    I will satisfy you with a long life.
    I will show you how I will save you.

Psalm 91:14–16

I look up toward the mountains.
    Where can I find help?
My help comes from the LORD,
    the maker of heaven and earth.
He will not let you fall.
    Your guardian will not fall asleep.
Indeed, the Guardian of Israel never rests or
        sleeps.
The LORD is your guardian.
The LORD is the shade over your right hand.
    The sun will not beat down on you during the
        day,
        nor will the moon at night.
The LORD guards you from every evil.
    He guards your life.

The LORD guards you as you come and go,
    now and forever.

Psalm 121

O Israel, put your hope in the LORD,
    because with the LORD there is mercy
        and with him there is unlimited forgiveness.
        He will rescue Israel from all its sins.

Psalm 130:7–8

Trust the LORD with all your heart,
    and do not rely on your own understanding.
In all your ways acknowledge him,
    and he will make your paths smooth.

Proverbs 3:5–6

Do not be afraid of sudden terror
    or of the destruction of wicked people when it
        comes.
    The LORD will be your confidence.
    He will keep your foot from getting caught.

Proverbs 3:25–26

Yet, the strength of those who wait with hope in
    the LORD
will be renewed.
    They will soar on wings like eagles.
        They will run and won't become weary.
        They will walk and won't grow tired.

Isaiah 40:31

Don't be afraid, because I am with you.
Don't be intimidated; I am your God.
  I will strengthen you.

Isaiah 41:10

Do not be afraid, because I have reclaimed you.
  I have called you by name; you are mine.
When you go through the sea, I am with you.
When you go through rivers, they will not
      sweep you away.
When you walk through fire, you will not be
      burned,
  and the flames will not harm you.

Isaiah 43:1–2

Even when you're old, I'll take care of you.
  Even when your hair turns gray, I'll support
        you.
I made you and will continue to care for you.
I'll support you and save you.

Isaiah 46:4

I know the plans that I have for you, declares the Lord.
They are plans for peace and not disaster, plans to give
you a future filled with hope. Then you will call to me.
You will come and pray to me, and I will hear you. When
you look for me, you will find me.

Jeremiah 29:11–13

I am going to gather the people from all the lands where I scattered them in my anger, fury, and terrifying wrath. I will bring them back to this place and make them live here securely. They will be my people, and I will be their God. I will give them the same attitude and the same purpose so that they will fear me as long as they live. This will be for their own good and for the good of their children. I will make an eternal promise to them that I will never stop blessing them. I will make them fear me so that they will never turn away from me. I will enjoy blessing them. With all my heart and soul I will faithfully plant them in this land.

Jeremiah 32:37–41

I will promise them peace. This promise will last forever. I will establish them, make them increase in number, and put my holy place among them permanently. My dwelling place will be with them. I will be their God, and they will be my people.

Ezekiel 37:26–27

I will look to the LORD.
I will wait for God to save me.
I will wait for my God to listen to me.

Micah 7:7

You are Peter, and I can guarantee that on this rock I will build my church. And the gates of hell will not overpower it. I will give you the keys of the kingdom of heaven. Whatever you imprison, God will imprison. And whatever you set free, God will set free.

Matthew 16:18−19

Jesus said, "I can guarantee this truth: Anyone who gave up his home, brothers, sisters, mother, father, children, or fields because of me and the Good News will certainly receive a hundred times as much here in this life. They will certainly receive homes, brothers, sisters, mothers, children and fields, along with persecutions. But in the world to come they will receive eternal life. But many who are first will be last, and the last will be first."

Mark 10:29−31

If you live in me and what I say lives in you, then ask for anything you want, and it will be yours. You give glory to my Father when you produce a lot of fruit and therefore show that you are my disciples.

John 15:7−8

He will continue to give you strength until the end so that no one can accuse you of anything on the day of our Lord Jesus Christ. God faithfully keeps his promises. He called you to be partners with his Son Jesus Christ our Lord.

1 Corinthians 1:8−9

I'm convinced that God, who began this good work in you, will carry it through to completion on the day of Christ Jesus.

Philippians 1:6

Christ means everything to me in this life, and when I die I'll have even more.

Philippians 1:21

We thank God because we have heard about your faith in Christ Jesus and your love for all of God's people. You have these because of the hope which is kept safe for you in heaven. Some time ago you heard about this hope in the Good News which is the message of truth.

Colossians 1:4–5

So don't lose your confidence. It will bring you a great reward. You need endurance so that after you have done what God wants you to do, you can receive what he has promised.

Hebrews 10:35–36

God's Word

Never stop reciting these teachings. You must think about them night and day so that you will faithfully do everything written in them. Only then will you prosper and succeed.

Joshua 1:8

How can a young person keep his life pure?
He can do it by holding on to your word.
I wholeheartedly searched for you.
Do not let me wander away from your
commandments.
I have treasured your promise in my heart
so that I may not sin against you.

Psalm 119:9–11

O LORD, your word is established in heaven
forever.

Psalm 119:89

Your word is a lamp for my feet
and a light for my path.

Psalm 119:105

Grass dries up,
and flowers wither,
but the word of our God will last forever.

Isaiah 40:8

The man whom God has sent speaks God's message. After all, God gives him the Spirit without limit.

John 3:34

Do everything without complaining or arguing. Then you will be blameless and innocent. You will be God's children without any faults among people who are crooked and corrupt. You will shine like stars among them in the world as you hold firmly to the word of life.

Philippians 2:14–16

Here is another reason why we never stop thanking God: When you received God's word from us, you realized it wasn't the word of humans. Instead, you accepted it for what it really is—the word of God. This word is at work in you believers.

1 Thessalonians 2:13

Every Scripture passage is inspired by God. All of them are useful for teaching, pointing out errors, correcting people, and training them for a life that has God's approval. They equip God's servants so that they are completely prepared to do good things.

2 Timothy 3:16–17

In the past God spoke to our ancestors at many different times and in many different ways through the prophets. In these last days he has spoken to us through his Son. God made his Son responsible for everything. His Son is the one through whom God made the universe.

Hebrews 1:1–2

God's word is living and active. It is sharper than any two-edged sword and cuts as deep as the place where soul and spirit meet, the place where joints and marrow meet. God's word judges a person's thoughts and intentions.

Hebrews 4:12

Hope for Eternal Life

Certainly, goodness and mercy will stay close to
    me all the days of my life,
    and I will remain in the LORD's house for days
      without end.

Psalm 23:6

You defend my integrity,
    and you set me in your presence forever.

Psalm 41:12

I will create a new heaven and a new earth.
    Past things will not be remembered.
    They will not come to mind.

Isaiah 65:17

When Jesus saw the crowds, he went up a moun-
    tain and sat down. His disciples came to
    him, and he began to teach them:
"Blessed are those who recognize they are spiritu-
    ally helpless.
    The kingdom of heaven belongs to them.
Blessed are those who mourn.
    They will be comforted.
Blessed are those who are gentle.
    They will inherit the earth.

Blessed are those who hunger and thirst for God's
approval.
They will be satisfied.
Blessed are those who show mercy.
They will be treated mercifully.
Blessed are those whose thoughts are pure.
They will see God.
Blessed are those who make peace.
They will be called God's children.
Blessed are those who are persecuted for doing
what God approves of.
The kingdom of heaven belongs to them.

"Blessed are you when people insult you,
persecute you,
lie, and say all kinds of evil things about you
because of me.
Rejoice and be glad because you have a great reward in heaven!
The prophets who lived before you were persecuted in these ways."

Matthew 5:1–12

Jesus said, "I can guarantee this truth: Anyone who gave
up his home, brothers, sisters, mother, father, children,
or fields because of me and the Good News will certainly
receive a hundred times as much here in this life. They
will certainly receive homes, brothers, sisters, mothers,
children and fields, along with persecutions. But in the
world to come they will receive eternal life. But many
who are first will be last, and the last will be first."

Mark 10:29–31

God loved the world this way: He gave his only Son so that everyone who believes in him will not die but will have eternal life.

John 3:16

Jesus answered her, "Everyone who drinks this water will become thirsty again. But those who drink the water that I will give them will never become thirsty again. In fact, the water I will give them will become in them a spring that gushes up to eternal life."

John 4:13

I can guarantee this truth: A time is coming (and is now here) when the dead will hear the voice of the Son of God and those who respond to it will live.

John 5:25

Don't work for food that spoils. Instead, work for the food that lasts into eternal life. This is the food the Son of Man will give you. After all, the Father has placed his seal of approval on him.

John 6:27

My flesh is true food, and my blood is true drink. Those who eat my flesh and drink my blood live in me, and I live in them. The Father who has life sent me, and I live because of the Father. So those who feed on me will live because of me. This is the bread that came from heaven. It is not like the bread your ancestors ate. They eventually died. Those who eat this bread will live forever.

John 6:55–58

Jesus said to her, "I am the one who brings people back to life, and I am life itself. Those who believe in me will live even if they die. Everyone who lives and believes in me will never die. Do you believe that?"

John 11:25−26

As sin ruled by bringing death, God's kindness would rule by bringing us his approval. This results in our living forever because of Jesus Christ our Lord.

Romans 5:21

Now you have been freed from sin and have become God's slaves. This results in a holy life and, finally, in everlasting life. The payment for sin is death, but the gift that God freely gives is everlasting life found in Christ Jesus our Lord.

Romans 6:22−23

As Scripture says:

"No eye has seen,
    no ear has heard,
        and no mind has imagined
            the things that God has prepared
                for those who love him."

God has revealed those things to us by his Spirit.

1 Corinthians 2:9−10

We know that if the life we live here on earth is ever taken down like a tent, we still have a building from

God. It is an eternal house in heaven that isn't made by human hands.

2 Corinthians 5:1

We can't allow ourselves to get tired of living the right way. Certainly, each of us will receive everlasting life at the proper time, if we don't give up.

Galatians 6:9

We were dead because of our failures, but he made us alive together with Christ. (It is God's kindness that saved you.) God has brought us back to life together with Christ Jesus and has given us a position in heaven with him. He did this through Christ Jesus out of his generosity to us in order to show his extremely rich kindness in the world to come.

Ephesians 2:5–7

Christ means everything to me in this life, and when I die I'll have even more.

Philippians 1:21

We thank God because we have heard about your faith in Christ Jesus and your love for all of God's people. You have these because of the hope which is kept safe for you in heaven. Some time ago you heard about this hope in the Good News which is the message of truth.

Colossians 1:4–5

From Paul, a servant of God and an apostle of Jesus Christ. I was sent to lead God's chosen people to faith and to the knowledge of the truth that leads to a godly life. My message is based on the confidence of eternal life. God, who never lies, promised this eternal life before the world began.

Titus 1:1–2

As a result, God in his kindness has given us his approval and we have become heirs who have the confidence that we have everlasting life.

Titus 3:7

The world and its evil desires are passing away. But the person who does what God wants lives forever.

1 John 2:17

Christ has given us the promise of eternal life.

1 John 2:25

This is the testimony: God has given us eternal life, and this life is found in his Son. The person who has the Son has this life. The person who doesn't have the Son of God doesn't have this life.

1 John 5:11–12

Let the person who has ears listen to what the Spirit says to the churches. I will give the privilege of eating from the tree of life, which stands in the paradise of God, to everyone who wins the victory.

Revelation 2:7

I heard a voice from heaven saying, "Write this: From now on those who die believing in the Lord are blessed."

Revelation 14:13

I saw a new heaven and a new earth, because the first heaven and earth had disappeared, and the sea was gone. Then I saw the holy city, New Jerusalem, coming down from God out of heaven, dressed like a bride ready for her husband. I heard a loud voice from the throne say, "God lives with humans! God will make his home with them, and they will be his people. God himself will be with them and be their God. He will wipe every tear from their eyes. There won't be any more death. There won't be any grief, crying, or pain, because the first things have disappeared."

Revelation 21:1–4

I'm coming soon! I will bring my reward with me to pay all people based on what they have done. I am the A and the Z, the first and the last, the beginning and the end.

Revelation 22:12–13

Hope for Living

Wait with hope for the LORD.
Be strong, and let your heart be courageous.
Yes, wait with hope for the LORD.

Psalm 27:14

Why are you discouraged, my soul?
Why are you so restless?
Put your hope in God,
because I will still praise him.
He is my savior and my God.

Psalm 42:5

My body and mind may waste away,
but God remains the foundation of my life
and my inheritance forever.

Psalm 73:26

The LORD is good.
His mercy endures forever.
His faithfulness endures throughout every
generation.

Psalm 100:5

Hallelujah!
Give thanks to the LORD because he is good,
  because his mercy endures forever.

                              Psalm 106:1

He has sent salvation to his people.
He has ordered that his promise should continue
    forever.

                              Psalm 111:9

Praise the LORD, all you nations!
Praise him, all you people of the world!
    His mercy toward us is powerful.
    The LORD's faithfulness endures forever.
Hallelujah!

                              Psalm 117

The LORD guards you as you come and go,
  now and forever.

                              Psalm 121:8

Blessed are those who receive help from the God
    of Jacob.
    Their hope rests on the LORD their God,
      who made heaven, earth,
        the sea, and everything in them.
    The LORD remains faithful forever.

                              Psalm 146:5–6

Yet, the strength of those who wait with hope in
the Lord
will be renewed.
They will soar on wings like eagles.
They will run and won't become weary.
They will walk and won't grow tired.

Isaiah 40:31

You will go out with joy and be led out in peace.
The mountains and the hills
will break into songs of joy in your presence,
and all the trees will clap their hands.
Cypress trees will grow where thornbushes grew.
Myrtle trees will grow where briars grew.
This will be a reminder of the Lord's name
and an everlasting sign that will never be
destroyed.

Isaiah 55:12–13

I know the plans that I have for you, declares the Lord.
They are plans for peace and not disaster, plans to give
you a future filled with hope. Then you will call to me.
You will come and pray to me, and I will hear you.
When you look for me, you will find me.

Jeremiah 29:11–13

The reason I can still find hope is that I keep this
one thing in mind:
the Lord's mercy.
We were not completely wiped out.

His compassion is never limited.
  It is new every morning.
  His faithfulness is great.
My soul can say, "The LORD is my lot in life.
  That is why I find hope in him."
The LORD is good to those who wait for him,
  to anyone who seeks help from him.

Lamentations 3:21–25

I will plant my people in the land.
  Those who are not loved I will call my loved
    ones.
  Those who are not my people I will call my
    people.
Then they will say, "You are our God!"

Hosea 2:23

The righteous person will live because of his
  faithfulness.

Habakkuk 2:4

I will set your captives free from the waterless pit
  because of the blood that sealed my promise to
    you.
Return to your fortress, you captives who have
  hope.
  Today I tell you that I will return to you double
    blessings.

Zechariah 9:11–12

A new day will dawn on us from above
because our God is loving and merciful.

Luke 1:78

What can we say about all of this? If God is for us, who can be against us? God didn't spare his own Son but handed him over to death for all of us. So he will also give us everything along with him. Who will accuse those whom God has chosen? God has approved of them. Who will condemn them? Christ has died, and more importantly, he was brought back to life. Christ has the highest position in heaven. Christ also intercedes for us. What will separate us from the love Christ has for us? Can trouble, distress, persecution, hunger, nakedness, danger, or violent death separate us from his love? As Scripture says:

> "We are being killed all day long because of you.
> We are thought of as sheep to be slaughtered."

The one who loves us gives us an overwhelming victory in all these difficulties. I am convinced that nothing can ever separate us from God's love which Christ Jesus our Lord shows us. We can't be separated by death or life, by angels or rulers, by anything in the present or anything in the future, by forces or powers in the world above or in the world below, or by anything else in creation.

Romans 8:31–39

I'm convinced that God, who began this good work in you, will carry it through to completion on the day of Christ Jesus.

Philippians 1:6

God wanted his people throughout the world to know the glorious riches of this mystery—which is Christ living in you, giving you the hope of glory.

Colossians 1:27

God our Father loved us and by his kindness gave us everlasting encouragement and good hope. Together with our Lord Jesus Christ, may he encourage and strengthen you to do and say everything that is good.

2 Thessalonians 2:16–17

Humble yourselves in the Lord's presence. Then he will give you a high position.

James 4:10

Hope for the Resurrection

Even though I walk through the dark valley of
death,
because you are with me, I fear no harm.
Your rod and your staff give me courage.

Psalm 23:4

This God is our God forever and ever.
He will lead us beyond death.

Psalm 48:14

Precious in the sight of the LORD
is the death of his faithful ones.

Psalm 116:15

He will swallow up death forever.
The Almighty LORD will wipe away tears from
every face,
and he will remove the disgrace of his people
from the whole earth.
The LORD has spoken.

Isaiah 25:8

Then people will see the Son of Man coming in clouds with great power and glory. He will send out his angels, and from every direction under the sky, they will gather those whom God has chosen.

Mark 13:26–27

The chief priest asked him again, "Are you the Messiah, the Son of the Blessed One?"

Jesus answered, "Yes, I am, and you will see the Son of Man in the highest position in heaven. He will be coming with the clouds of heaven."

Mark 14:61–62

The one who sent me doesn't want me to lose any of those he gave me. He wants me to bring them back to life on the last day.

John 6:39

Don't be troubled. Believe in God, and believe in me. My Father's house has many rooms. If that were not true, would I have told you that I'm going to prepare a place for you? If I go to prepare a place for you, I will come again. Then I will bring you into my presence so that you will be where I am.

John 14:1–3

If we've become united with him in a death like his, certainly we will also be united with him when we come back to life as he did.

Romans 6:5

Christ must rule until God has put every enemy under his control. The last enemy he will destroy is death.

1 Corinthians 15:25–26

I'm telling you a mystery. Not all of us will die, but we will all be changed. It will happen in an instant, in a split second at the sound of the last trumpet. Indeed, that trumpet will sound, and then the dead will come back to life. They will be changed so that they can live forever. This body that decays must be changed into a body that cannot decay. This mortal body must be changed into a body that will live forever. When this body that decays is changed into a body that cannot decay, and this mortal body is changed into a body that will live forever, then the teaching of Scripture will come true:

> "Death is turned into victory!
>   Death, where is your victory?
>   Death, where is your sting?"

Sin gives death its sting, and God's standards give sin its power. Thank God that he gives us the victory through our Lord Jesus Christ.

1 Corinthians 15:51–57

Faith knows the power that his coming back to life gives and what it means to share his suffering. In this way I'm becoming like him in his death, with the confidence that I'll come back to life from the dead.

Philippians 3:10–11

We believe that Jesus died and came back to life. We also believe that, through Jesus, God will bring back those who have died. They will come back with Jesus.

1 Thessalonians 4:14

The Lord will come from heaven with a command, with the voice of the archangel, and with the trumpet call of God. First, the dead who believed in Christ will come back to life. Then, together with them, we who are still alive will be taken in the clouds to meet the Lord in the air. In this way we will always be with the Lord. So then, comfort each other with these words!

1 Thessalonians 4:16–18

It was not God's intention that we experience his anger but that we obtain salvation through our Lord Jesus Christ. He died for us so that, whether we are awake in this life or asleep in death, we will live together with him. Therefore, encourage each other and strengthen one another as you are doing.

1 Thessalonians 5:9–11

But now, at the end of the ages, he has appeared once to remove sin by his sacrifice. People die once, and after that they are judged. Likewise, Christ was sacrificed once to take away the sins of humanity, and after that he will appear a second time. This time he will not deal with sin, but he will save those who eagerly wait for him.

Hebrews 9:26–28

The Presence of the Father

Don't be afraid of them, because the Lord your God is with you. He is a great and awe-inspiring God.

Deuteronomy 7:21

Be strong and courageous. Don't tremble! Don't be afraid of them! The Lord your God is the one who is going with you. He won't abandon you or leave you.

Deuteronomy 31:6

I have commanded you, "Be strong and courageous! Don't tremble or be terrified, because the Lord your God is with you wherever you go."

Joshua 1:9

You won't fight this battle. Instead, take your position, stand still, and see the victory of the Lord for you, Judah and Jerusalem. Don't be frightened or terrified. Tomorrow go out to face them. The Lord is with you.

2 Chronicles 20:17

Your kindness is so great!
　You reserve it for those who fear you.
　　Adam's descendants watch
　　　as you show it to those who take refuge in
　　　　you.
　You hide them in the secret place of your
　　　presence
　from those who scheme against them.
　You keep them in a shelter,
　　safe from quarrelsome tongues.

Psalm 31:19–20

The Messenger of the LORD camps around those
　　who fear him,
　and he rescues them.

Psalm 34:7

The LORD's eyes are on righteous people.
His ears hear their cry for help.

Psalm 34:15

Righteous people cry out.
The LORD hears and rescues them from all their
　　troubles.

Psalm 34:17

The LORD is near to those whose hearts are
　　humble.
He saves those whose spirits are crushed.

Psalm 34:18

But I wait with hope for you, O Lord.
You will answer, O Lord, my God.

Psalm 38:15

There is a river
  whose streams bring joy to the city of God,
    the holy place where the Most High lives.
God is in that city.
  It cannot fall.
    God will help it at the break of dawn.

Psalm 46:4–5

Our God will come and will not remain silent.
  A devouring fire is in front of him
    and a raging storm around him.

Psalm 50:3

Morning, noon, and night I complain and groan,
  and he listens to my voice.

Psalm 55:17

You make the path of life known to me.
  Complete joy is in your presence.
    Pleasures are by your side forever.

Psalm 116:11

He will not let you fall.
  Your guardian will not fall asleep.
Indeed, the Guardian of Israel never rests or sleeps.

Psalm 121:3–4

How precious are your thoughts concerning me,
O God!
How vast in number they are!
If I try to count them,
there would be more of them than there are
grains of sand.
When I wake up, I am still with you.

Psalm 139:17–18

Don't you know?
Haven't you heard?
The eternal God, the LORD, the Creator of the
ends of the earth,
doesn't grow tired or become weary.
His understanding is beyond reach.

Isaiah 40:28

Do not be afraid, because I am with you.
I will bring your descendants from the east
and gather you from the west.
I will say to the north, "Give them up,"
and to the south, "Do not keep them."
Bring my sons from far away
and my daughters from the ends of the earth.

Isaiah 43:5–6

The High and Lofty One lives forever, and his
   name is holy.
This is what he says:
   I live in a high and holy place.
      But I am with those who are crushed and
         humble.
         I will renew the spirit of those who are
            humble
            and the courage of those who are
               crushed.

Isaiah 57:15

I know the plans that I have for you, declares the Lord.
They are plans for peace and not disaster, plans to give
you a future filled with hope. Then you will call to me.
You will come and pray to me, and I will hear you.
When you look for me, you will find me.

Jeremiah 29:11−13

I will promise them peace. This promise will last forever.
I will establish them, make them increase in number,
and put my holy place among them permanently. My
dwelling place will be with them. I will be their God,
and they will be my people.

Ezekiel 37:26−27

Let's return to the LORD.
   Even though he has torn us to pieces,
      he will heal us.
   Even though he has wounded us,

he will bandage our wounds.
After two days he will revive us.
On the third day he will raise us
so that we may live in his presence.
Let's learn about the LORD.
Let's get to know the LORD.
He will come to us as sure as the morning
comes.
He will come to us like the autumn rains and
the spring rains
that water the ground.

Hosea 6:1–3

"Break new ground.
Plant righteousness,
and harvest the fruit that your loyalty will
produce for me."
It's time to seek the LORD!
When he comes, he will rain righteousness on
you.

Hosea 10:12

On that day Jerusalem will be told,
"Do not be afraid, Zion!
Do not lose courage!"
The LORD your God is with you.
He is a hero who saves you.
He happily rejoices over you,
renews you with his love,
and celebrates over you with shouts of
joy.

Zephaniah 3:16–17

You are Peter, and I can guarantee that on this rock I will build my church. And the gates of hell will not overpower it. I will give you the keys of the kingdom of heaven. Whatever you imprison, God will imprison. And whatever you set free, God will set free.

Matthew 16:18–19

Come close to God, and he will come close to you.

James 4:8

"I am the A and the Z," says the Lord God, the one who is, the one who was, and the one who is coming, the Almighty.

Revelation 1:8

The Presence of the Son

When Jesus came near, he spoke to them. He said, "All authority in heaven and on earth has been given to me. So wherever you go, make disciples of all nations: Baptize them in the name of the Father, and of the Son, and of the Holy Spirit. Teach them to do everything I have commanded you. And remember that I am always with you until the end of time."

Matthew 28:18–20

I will not leave you all alone. I will come back to you. In a little while the world will no longer see me, but you will see me. You will live because I live. On that day you will know that I am in my Father and that you are in me and that I am in you.

John 14:18–20

Whoever knows and obeys my commandments is the person who loves me. Those who love me will have my Father's love, and I, too, will love them and show myself to them.

John 14:21

Jesus answered him, "Those who love me will do what I say. My Father will love them, and we will go to them and make our home with them."

John 14:23

I am the vine. You are the branches. Those who live in me while I live in them will produce a lot of fruit. But you can't produce anything without me.

John 15:5

The Presence
of the Holy Spirit

I will give you a new heart and put a new spirit in you. I will remove your stubborn hearts and give you obedient hearts. I will put my Spirit in you. I will enable you to live by my laws, and you will obey my rules. Then you will live in the land that I gave your ancestors. You will be my people, and I will be your God.

Ezekiel 36:26–28

[The LORD said to his people]
"After this, I will pour my Spirit on everyone.
   Your sons and daughters will prophesy.
   Your old men will dream dreams.
   Your young men will see visions.
In those days I will pour my Spirit on servants,
   on both men and women.
     I will work miracles in the sky and on the
       earth:
       blood, fire, and clouds of smoke.
       The sun will become dark,

and the moon will become as red as
blood
before the terrifying day of the
Lord comes."
Then whoever calls on the name of the Lord will
be saved.
Those who escape will be on Mount Zion and
in Jerusalem.
Among the survivors will be those whom the
Lord calls,
as the Lord has promised.

Joel 2:28–32

Then he replied, "This is the word the Lord spoke to
Zerubbabel: You won't succeed by might or by power,
but by my Spirit, says the Lord of Armies."

Zechariah 4:6

I baptize you with water so that you will change the
way you think and act. But the one who comes after
me is more powerful than I. I am not worthy to remove
his sandals. He will baptize you with the Holy Spirit
and fire.

Matthew 3:11

When you are put on trial in synagogues or in front of
rulers and authorities, don't worry about how you will
defend yourselves or what you will say. At that time the
Holy Spirit will teach you what you must say.

Luke 12:11

The man whom God has sent speaks God's message. After all, God gives him the Spirit without limit.

John 3:34

I will ask the Father, and he will give you another helper who will be with you forever. That helper is the Spirit of Truth. The world cannot accept him, because it doesn't see or know him. You know him, because he lives with you and will be in you.

John 14:16−17

Peter answered them, "All of you must turn to God and change the way you think and act, and each of you must be baptized in the name of Jesus Christ so that your sins will be forgiven. Then you will receive the Holy Spirit as a gift. This promise belongs to you and to your children and to everyone who is far away. It belongs to everyone who worships the Lord our God."

Acts 2:38−39

At the same time the Spirit also helps us in our weakness, because we don't know how to pray for what we need. But the Spirit intercedes along with our groans that cannot be expressed in words. The one who searches our hearts knows what the Spirit has in mind. The Spirit intercedes for God's people the way God wants him to.

Romans 8:26−27

Don't you know that your body is a temple that belongs to the Holy Spirit? The Holy Spirit, whom you received from God, lives in you. You don't belong to yourselves. You were bought for a price. So bring glory to God in the way you use your body.

1 Corinthians 6:19–20

Christ gives us confidence about you in God's presence. By ourselves we are not qualified in any way to claim that we can do anything. Rather, God makes us qualified. He has also qualified us to be ministers of a new promise, a spiritual promise, not a written one. Clearly, what was written brings death, but the Spirit brings life.

2 Corinthians 3:4–6

This Lord is the Spirit. Wherever the Lord's Spirit is, there is freedom. As all of us reflect the Lord's glory with faces that are not covered with veils, we are being changed into his image with ever-increasing glory. This comes from the Lord, who is the Spirit.

2 Corinthians 3:17–18

Christ paid the price to free us from the curse that God's laws bring by becoming cursed instead of us. Scripture says, "Everyone who is hung on a tree is cursed." Christ paid the price so that the blessing promised to Abraham would come to all the people of the world through Jesus Christ and we would receive the promised Spirit through faith.

Galatians 3:13–14

You heard and believed the message of truth, the Good News that he has saved you. In him you were sealed with the Holy Spirit whom he promised. This Holy Spirit is the guarantee that we will receive our inheritance. We have this guarantee until we are set free to belong to him. God receives praise and glory for this.

Ephesians 1:13−14

That is why you are no longer foreigners and outsiders but citizens together with God's people and members of God's family. You are built on the foundation of the apostles and prophets. Christ Jesus himself is the cornerstone. In him all the parts of the building fit together and grow into a holy temple in the Lord. Through him you, also, are being built in the Spirit together with others into a place where God lives.

Ephesians 2:19−22

I, a prisoner in the Lord, encourage you to live the kind of life which proves that God has called you. Be humble and gentle in every way. Be patient with each other and lovingly accept each other. Through the peace that ties you together, do your best to maintain the unity that the Spirit gives. There is one body and one Spirit. In the same way you were called to share one hope. There is one Lord, one faith, one baptism, one God and Father of all, who is over everything, through everything, and in everything.

Ephesians 4:1−6

Don't give God's Holy Spirit any reason to be upset with you. He has put his seal on you for the day you will be set free from the world of sin.

Ephesians 4:30

Once you lived in the dark, but now the Lord has filled you with light. Live as children who have light.

Ephesians 5:8

Also take salvation as your helmet and the word of God as the sword that the Spirit supplies.

Ephesians 6:17

Live as citizens who reflect the Good News about Christ. Then, whether I come to see you or whether I stay away, I'll hear all about you. I'll hear that you are firmly united in spirit, united in fighting for the faith that the Good News brings.

Philippians 1:27

God revealed to the prophets that the things they had spoken were not for their own benefit but for yours. What the prophets had spoken, the Holy Spirit, who was sent from heaven, has now made known to you by those who spread the Good News among you. These are things that even the angels want to look into.

1 Peter 1:12

However, you are chosen people, a royal priesthood, a holy nation, people who belong to God. You were chosen to tell about the excellent qualities of God, who called you out of darkness into his marvelous light. Once you were not God's people, but now you are. Once you were not shown mercy, but now you have been shown mercy.

1 Peter 2:9–10

First, you must understand this: No prophecy in Scripture is a matter of one's own interpretation. No prophecy ever originated from humans. Instead, it was given by the Holy Spirit as humans spoke under God's direction.

2 Peter 1:20–21

I'm writing to you, dear children, because your sins are forgiven through Christ. I'm writing to you, fathers, because you know Christ who has existed from the beginning. I'm writing to you, young people, because you have won the victory over the evil one. I've written to you, children, because you know the Father. I've written to you, fathers, because you know Christ, who has existed from the beginning. I've written to you, young people, because you are strong and God's word lives in you. You have won the victory over the evil one.

1 John 2:12–14

Those who obey Christ's commandments live in God, and God lives in them. We know that he lives in us because he has given us the Spirit.

1 John 3:24

Dear children, you belong to God. So you have won the victory over these people, because the one who is in you is greater than the one who is in the world.

1 John 4:4

No one has ever seen God. If we love each other, God lives in us, and his love is perfected in us. We know that we live in him and he lives in us because he has given us his Spirit.

1 John 4:12–13

I will make everyone who wins the victory a pillar in the temple of my God. They will never leave it again. I will write on them the name of my God, the name of the city of my God (the New Jerusalem coming down out of heaven from my God), and my new name.

Revelation 3:12

You bought people with your blood to be God's own.
   They are from every tribe, language, people, and nation.
You made them a kingdom and priests for our God.
   They will rule as kings on the earth.

Revelation 5:9–10

The angel showed me a river filled with the water of life, as clear as crystal. It was flowing from the throne of God and the lamb. Between the street of the city and the river there was a tree of life visible from both sides. It produced 12 kinds of fruit. Each month had its own fruit. The leaves of the tree will heal the nations. There will no longer be any curse. The throne of God and the lamb will be in the city. His servants will worship him and see his face. His name will be on their foreheads. There will be no more night, and they will not need any light from lamps or the sun because the Lord God will shine on them. They will rule as kings forever and ever.

Revelation 22:1–5

The Return of Christ

Then people will see the Son of Man coming in clouds with great power and glory. He will send out his angels, and from every direction under the sky, they will gather those whom God has chosen.

Mark 13:26–27

We, however, are citizens of heaven. We look forward to the Lord Jesus Christ coming from heaven as our Savior. Through his power to bring everything under his authority, he will change our humble bodies and make them like his glorified body.

Philippians 3:20–21

He will continue to give you strength until the end so that no one can accuse you of anything on the day of our Lord Jesus Christ. God faithfully keeps his promises. He called you to be partners with his Son Jesus Christ our Lord.

1 Corinthians 1:8–9

May the God who gives peace make you holy in every way. May he keep your whole being—spirit, soul, and body—blameless when our Lord Jesus Christ comes. The one who calls you is faithful, and he will do this.

1 Thessalonians 5:23–24

Then the man of sin will be revealed and the Lord Jesus will destroy him by what he says. When the Lord Jesus comes, his appearance will put an end to this man.

2 Thessalonians 2:8

You, too, must be patient. Don't give up hope. The Lord will soon be here.

James 5:8

The Lord isn't slow to do what he promised, as some people think. Rather, he is patient for your sake. He doesn't want to destroy anyone but wants all people to have an opportunity to turn to him and change the way they think and act.

2 Peter 3:9

Now, dear children, live in Christ. Then, when he appears we will have confidence, and when he comes we won't turn from him in shame. If you know that Christ has God's approval, you also know that everyone who does what God approves of has been born from God.

1 John 2:28–29

Look! He is coming in the clouds.
    Every eye will see him,
        even those who pierced him.
    Every tribe on earth will mourn because of
        him.
        This is true. Amen.

Revelation 1:7

I'm coming soon! I will bring my reward with me to pay all people based on what they have done. I am the A and the Z, the first and the last, the beginning and the end.

Revelation 22:12–13

God Promises Help
When I Feel . . .

Anger

Let go of anger, and leave rage behind.
    Do not be preoccupied.
        It only leads to evil.
Evildoers will be cut off from their inheritance,
    but those who wait with hope for the Lord will
        inherit the land.

Psalm 37:8–9

Even though I walk into the middle of trouble,
    you guard my life against the anger of my
        enemies.
You stretch out your hand,
    and your right hand saves me.

Psalm 138:7

But I tell everyone who is listening: Love your enemies.
Be kind to those who hate you. Bless those who curse
you. Pray for those who insult you. . . .

Love your enemies, help them. . . . Then you will
have a great reward. You will be the children of the
Most High God. After all, he is kind to unthankful and
evil people.

Luke 6:27–28, 35

As much as it is possible, live in peace with everyone. Don't take revenge, dear friends. Instead, let God's anger take care of it. After all, Scripture says, "I alone have the right to take revenge. I will pay back, says the Lord." But,

> "If your enemy is hungry, feed him.
>> If he is thirsty, give him a drink.
>>> If you do this, you will make him feel guilty
>>> and ashamed."

Don't let evil conquer you, but conquer evil with good.

Romans 12:18–21

Be angry without sinning. Don't go to bed angry. Don't give the devil any opportunity to work.

Get rid of your bitterness, hot tempers, anger, loud quarreling, cursing, and hatred. Be kind to each other, sympathetic, forgiving each other as God has forgiven you through Christ.

Ephesians 4:26–27, 31–32

Therefore, put to death whatever is worldly in you: your sexual sin, perversion, passion, lust, and greed (which is the same thing as worshiping wealth). It is because of these sins that God's anger comes on those who refuse to obey him. You used to live that kind of sinful life. Also get rid of your anger, hot tempers, hatred, cursing, obscene language, and all similar sins.

As holy people whom God has chosen and loved, be sympathetic, kind, humble, gentle, and patient. Put up with each other, and forgive each other if anyone has a complaint. Forgive as the Lord forgave you.

Colossians 3:5–8, 12–13

It was not God's intention that we experience his anger but that we obtain salvation through our Lord Jesus Christ. He died for us so that, whether we are awake in this life or asleep in death, we will live together with him. Therefore, encourage each other and strengthen one another as you are doing.

1 Thessalonians 5:9–11

Finally, everyone must live in harmony, be sympathetic, love each other, have compassion, and be humble. Don't pay people back with evil for the evil they do to you, or ridicule those who ridicule you. Instead, bless them, because you were called to inherit a blessing.

> "People who want to live a full life and enjoy
>   good days
>   must keep their tongues from saying evil things,
>   and their lips from speaking deceitful things.
> They must turn away from evil and do good.
>   They must seek peace and pursue it.
> The Lord's eyes are on those who do what he
>   approves.
>   His ears hear their prayer.
> The Lord confronts those who do evil."

1 Peter 3:8–12

Anxiety

Come to me, all who are tired from carrying heavy loads, and I will give you rest. Place my yoke over your shoulders, and learn from me, because I am gentle and humble. Then you will find rest for yourselves because my yoke is easy and my burden is light.

Matthew 11:28–30

I'm leaving you peace. I'm giving you my peace. I don't give you the kind of peace that the world gives. So don't be troubled or cowardly.

John 14:27

Through the peace that ties you together, do your best to maintain the unity that the Spirit gives.

Ephesians 4:3

good

Always be joyful in the Lord! I'll say it again: Be joyful! Let everyone know how considerate you are. The Lord is near. Never worry about anything. But in every situation let God know what you need in prayers and requests while giving thanks. Then God's peace, which goes beyond anything we can imagine, will guard your thoughts and emotions through Christ Jesus.

Philippians 4:4–7

Finally, brothers and sisters, keep your thoughts on whatever is right or deserves praise: things that are true, honorable, fair, pure, acceptable, or commendable. Practice what you've learned and received from me, what you heard and saw me do. Then the God who gives this peace will be with you.

Philippians 4:8–9

Good will, mercy, and peace from God the Father and Christ Jesus our Lord are yours!

1 Timothy 1:2

Good will and peace from God the Father and from Christ Jesus our Savior are yours!

Titus 1:4

Turn all your anxiety over to God because he cares for you.

1 Peter 5:7

Confusion

Trust the LORD with all your heart,
    and do not rely on your own understanding.
In all your ways acknowledge him,
    and he will make your paths smooth.

Proverbs 3:5–6

At the same time the Spirit also helps us in our weakness, because we don't know how to pray for what we need. But the Spirit intercedes along with our groans that cannot be expressed in words. The one who searches our hearts knows what the Spirit has in mind. The Spirit intercedes for God's people the way God wants him to.

Romans 8:26–27

Through the blood of his Son, we are set free from our sins. God forgives our failures because of his overflowing kindness. He poured out his kindness by giving us every kind of wisdom and insight when he revealed the mystery of his plan to us. He had decided to do this through Christ.

Ephesians 1:7–9

God didn't give us a cowardly spirit but a spirit of power, love, and good judgment.

2 Timothy 1:7

If any of you needs wisdom to know what you should do, you should ask God, and he will give it to you. God is generous to everyone and doesn't find fault with them.

James 1:5

Wherever there is jealousy and rivalry, there is disorder and every kind of evil. However, the wisdom that comes from above is first of all pure. Then it is peaceful, gentle, obedient, filled with mercy and good deeds, impartial, and sincere. A harvest that has God's approval comes from the peace planted by peacemakers.

James 3:16–18

Discouragement

Even if my father and mother abandon me,
the LORD will take care of me.

Psalm 27:10

You crown the year with your goodness,
and richness overflows wherever you are.
The pastures in the desert overflow with
richness.
The hills are surrounded with joy.

Psalm 65:11–12

With my mouth I will give many thanks to the
LORD.
I will praise him among many people,
because he stands beside needy people
to save them from those who would condemn them to death.

Psalm 109:30–31

If you give some of your own food to feed those
      who are hungry
   and to satisfy the needs of those who are
      humble,
then your light will rise in the dark,
   and your darkness will become as bright as the
      noonday sun.

Isaiah 58:10

You know about the kindness of our Lord Jesus Christ.
He was rich, yet for your sake he became poor in order
to make you rich through his poverty.

2 Corinthians 8:9

Praise the God and Father of our Lord Jesus Christ!
Through Christ, God has blessed us with every spiritual
blessing that heaven has to offer.

Ephesians 1:3

I'm asking God to give you a gift from the wealth of his
glory. I pray that he would give you inner strength and
power through his Spirit.

Ephesians 3:16

God wanted his people throughout the world to know
the glorious riches of this mystery—which is Christ
living in you, giving you the hope of glory.

Colossians 1:27

I want you to know how hard I work for you, for the people of Laodicea, and for people I have never met. Because they are united in love, I work so that they may be encouraged by all the riches that come from a complete understanding of Christ. He is the mystery of God.

Colossians 2:1–2

Dissatisfaction

I will proclaim the name of the LORD.
Give our God the greatness he deserves!
 He is a rock.
  What he does is perfect.
   All his ways are fair.
He is a faithful God, who does no wrong.
 He is honorable and reliable.

Deuteronomy 32:3–4

Yet, the LORD is enthroned forever.
 He has set up his throne for judgment.
 He alone judges the world with righteousness.
 He judges its people fairly.
The LORD is a stronghold for the oppressed,
 a stronghold in times of trouble.
Those who know your name trust you, O LORD,
 because you have never deserted those who seek
  your help.

Psalm 9:7–10

The decisions of the LORD are true.
   They are completely fair.
   They are more desirable than gold, even the finest gold.
   They are sweeter than honey, even the drippings
      from a honeycomb.
   As your servant I am warned by them.
      There is a great reward in following them.

Psalm 19:9–11

Say to the nations, "The LORD rules as king!"
The earth stands firm; it cannot be moved.
He will judge people fairly.

Psalm 96:10

The LORD does what is right and fair
   for all who are oppressed.

Psalm 103:6

The LORD is fair in all his ways
   and faithful in everything he does.

Psalm 145:17

The things you do are spectacular and amazing,
    Lord God Almighty.
The way you do them is fair and true, King of the
    Nations.

Lord, who won't fear and praise your name?
    You are the only holy one,
        and all the nations will come to worship you
            because they know about your fair
                judgments.

Revelation 15:3–4

Doubt

Be strong and courageous. Don't tremble! Don't be afraid of them! The Lord your God is the one who is going with you. He won't abandon you or leave you.

Deuteronomy 31:6

I will proclaim the name of the Lord.
Give our God the greatness he deserves!
   He is a rock.
      What he does is perfect.
         All his ways are fair.
He is a faithful God, who does no wrong.
   He is honorable and reliable.

Deuteronomy 32:3–4

The Lord is my inheritance and my cup.
   You are the one who determines my destiny.
   Your boundary lines mark out pleasant places
      for me.
Indeed, my inheritance is something beautiful.

Psalm 16:5–6

The LORD is good.
    His mercy endures forever.
    His faithfulness endures throughout every
        generation.

Psalm 100:5

Praise the LORD, all you nations!
Praise him, all you people of the world!
    His mercy toward us is powerful.
    The LORD's faithfulness endures forever.
Hallelujah!

Psalm 117

The LORD is fair in all his ways
    and faithful in everything he does.

Psalm 145:17

Blessed are those who receive help from the God
    of Jacob.
    Their hope rests on the LORD their God,
        who made heaven, earth,
            the sea, and everything in them.
    The LORD remains faithful forever.

Psalm 146:5–6

Justice will be the belt around his waist.
Faithfulness will be the belt around his hips.

Isaiah 11:5

Can a woman forget her nursing child?
Will she have no compassion on the child from
    her womb?
Although mothers may forget,
  I will not forget you.

Isaiah 49:15

"The mountains may move, and the hills may
    shake,
  but my kindness will never depart from you.
    My promise of peace will never change,"
      says the LORD, who has compassion on
      you.

Isaiah 54:10

The reason I can still find hope is that I keep this
    one thing in mind:
  the LORD's mercy.
    We were not completely wiped out.
    His compassion is never limited.
      It is new every morning.
      His faithfulness is great.
    My soul can say, "The LORD is my lot in life.
    That is why I find hope in him."
    The LORD is good to those who wait for him,
    to anyone who seeks help from him.

Lamentations 3:21–25

Jesus said to them, "Have faith in God! I can guarantee
this truth: This is what will be done for someone who

doesn't doubt but believes what he says will happen: He can say to this mountain, 'Be uprooted and thrown into the sea,' and it will be done for him. That's why I tell you to have faith that you have already received whatever you pray for, and it will be yours."

Mark 11:22–24

He will continue to give you strength until the end so that no one can accuse you of anything on the day of our Lord Jesus Christ. God faithfully keeps his promises. He called you to be partners with his Son Jesus Christ our Lord.

1 Corinthians 1:8–9

There isn't any temptation that you have experienced which is unusual for humans. God, who faithfully keeps his promises, will not allow you to be tempted beyond your power to resist. But when you are tempted, he will also give you the ability to endure the temptation as your way of escape.

1 Corinthians 10:13

In every way we're troubled, but we aren't crushed by our troubles. We're frustrated, but we don't give up. We're persecuted, but we're not abandoned. We're captured, but we're not killed.

2 Corinthians 4:8–9

I'm convinced that God, who began this good work in you, will carry it through to completion on the day of Christ Jesus.

Philippians 1:6

May the God who gives peace make you holy in every way. May he keep your whole being—spirit, soul, and body—blameless when our Lord Jesus Christ comes. The one who calls you is faithful, and he will do this.

1 Thessalonians 5:23–24

This is a statement that can be trusted:

If we have died with him, we will live with him.
If we endure, we will rule with him.
If we disown him, he will disown us.
If we are unfaithful, he remains faithful
    because he cannot be untrue to himself.

2 Timothy 2:11–13

We have been sprinkled with his blood to free us from a guilty conscience, and our bodies have been washed with clean water. So we must continue to come to him with a sincere heart and strong faith. We must continue to hold firmly to our declaration of faith. The one who made the promise is faithful.

Hebrews 10:22–23

Those who suffer because that is God's will for them must entrust themselves to a faithful creator and continue to do what is good.

1 Peter 4:19

The one sitting on the throne said, "I am making everything new." He said, "Write this: 'These words are faithful and true.'"

Revelation 21:5

Fear

Don't be afraid of them, because the LORD your God is with you. He is a great and awe-inspiring God.

Deuteronomy 7:21

> Even though I walk through the dark valley of death,
>> because you are with me, I fear no harm.
>>> Your rod and your staff give me courage.

Psalm 23:4

The LORD is my light and my salvation.
  Who is there to fear?
The LORD is my life's fortress.
  Who is there to be afraid of?

Psalm 27:1

The LORD of Armies is with us.
The God of Jacob is our stronghold.

Psalm 46:7

Do not be afraid, because I have reclaimed you.
   I have called you by name; you are mine.
When you go through the sea, I am with you.
When you go through rivers, they will not
      sweep you away.
When you walk through fire, you will not be
      burned,
   and the flames will not harm you.

Isaiah 43:1–2

He promised to rescue us from our enemies'
      power
   so that we could serve him without fear
      by being holy and honorable as long as we
      live.

Luke 1:74–75

I'm leaving you peace. I'm giving you my peace. I don't give you the kind of peace that the world gives. So don't be troubled or cowardly.

John 14:27

God didn't give us a cowardly spirit but a spirit of power, love, and good judgment.

2 Timothy 1:7

So don't lose your confidence. It will bring you a great reward. You need endurance so that after you have done what God wants you to do, you can receive what he has promised.

Hebrews 10:35–36

The Lord is my helper.
I will not be afraid.
What can mortals do to me?

Hebrews 13:5–6

No fear exists where his love is. Rather, perfect love gets rid of fear, because fear involves punishment. The person who lives in fear doesn't have perfect love.

1 John 4:18

Don't be afraid of what you are going to suffer. The devil is going to throw some of you into prison so that you may be tested. Your suffering will go on for ten days. Be faithful until death, and I will give you the crown of life.

Revelation 2:10

Loneliness

Be strong and courageous. Don't tremble! Don't be afraid of them! The LORD your God is the one who is going with you. He won't abandon you or leave you.

Deuteronomy 31:6

You make the path of life known to me.
Complete joy is in your presence.
Pleasures are by your side forever.

Psalm 16:11

Even if my father and mother abandon me,
the LORD will take care of me.

Psalm 27:10

The LORD is near to those whose hearts are
humble.
He saves those whose spirits are crushed.

Psalm 34:18

The God who is in his holy dwelling place
  is the father of the fatherless and the defender
    of widows.
God places lonely people in families.
  He leads prisoners out of prison into produc-
    tive lives,
    but rebellious people must live in an unpro-
      ductive land.

Psalm 68:5–6

Weariness

Don't you know?
  Haven't you heard?
The eternal God, the LORD, the Creator of the
    ends of the earth,
  doesn't grow tired or become weary.
    His understanding is beyond reach.
He gives strength to those who grow tired
  and increases the strength of those who are
    weak.
Even young people grow tired and become weary,
  and young men will stumble and fall.
Yet, the strength of those who wait with hope in
    the LORD
  will be renewed.
    They will soar on wings like eagles.
      They will run and won't become weary.
      They will walk and won't grow tired.

                                    Isaiah 40:28–31

The LORD will continually guide you
    and satisfy you even in sun-baked places.
He will strengthen your bones.
    You will become like a watered garden
        and like a spring whose water does not stop
            flowing.

                                    Isaiah 58:11

Worry

Don't be afraid of them, because the LORD your God is with you. He is a great and awe-inspiring God.

Deuteronomy 7:21

Even though I walk into the middle of trouble,
  you guard my life against the anger of my
    enemies.
You stretch out your hand,
  and your right hand saves me.

Psalm 138:7

Gullible people kill themselves because of their
    turning away.
Fools destroy themselves because of their
    indifference.
But whoever listens to me will live without
    worry
  and will be free from the dread of disaster.

Proverbs 1:32–33

This is what the Almighty LORD says:
  I am going to lay a rock in Zion,
    a rock that has been tested,
    a precious cornerstone,
    a solid foundation.
      Whoever believes in him will not worry.

Isaiah 28:16

Break out into shouts of joy, ruins of Jerusalem.
  The LORD will comfort his people.
    He will reclaim Jerusalem.
  The LORD will show his holy power to all the
    nations.
All the ends of the earth will see the salvation of
  our God.

Isaiah 52:9–10

Don't ever worry and say, "What are we going to eat?"
or "What are we going to drink?" or "What are we going
to wear?" Everyone is concerned about these things,
and your heavenly Father certainly knows you need all
of them. But first, be concerned about his kingdom and
what has his approval. Then all these things will be provided for you.

Matthew 6:31–33

But nothing is impossible for God.

Luke 1:37

When you are put on trial in synagogues or in front of rulers and authorities, don't worry about how you will defend yourselves or what you will say. At that time the Holy Spirit will teach you what you must say.

Luke 12:11

Then Jesus said to his disciples, "So I tell you to stop worrying about what you will eat or wear. Life is more than food, and the body is more than clothes. Consider the crows. They don't plant or harvest. They don't even have a storeroom or a barn. Yet, God feeds them. You are worth much more than birds."

Luke 12:22–24

That's the way God clothes the grass in the field. Today it's alive, and tomorrow it's thrown into an incinerator. So how much more will he clothe you people who have so little faith?

Luke 12:28

Glory belongs to God, whose power is at work in us. By this power he can do infinitely more than we can ask or imagine. Glory belongs to God in the church and in Christ Jesus for all time and eternity! Amen.

Ephesians 3:20–21

Always be joyful in the Lord! I'll say it again: Be joyful! Let everyone know how considerate you are. The Lord is near. Never worry about anything. But in every situation let God know what you need in prayers and requests while giving thanks. Then God's peace, which goes beyond anything we can imagine, will guard your thoughts and emotions through Christ Jesus.

Philippians 4:4–7

God Promises That I Can
Stand Against . . .

Death

Even though I walk through the dark valley of
  death,
  because you are with me, I fear no harm.
  Your rod and your staff give me courage.

Psalm 23:4

You defend my integrity,
  and you set me in your presence forever.

Psalm 41:12

This God is our God forever and ever.
  He will lead us beyond death.

Psalm 48:14

Precious in the sight of the LORD
  is the death of his faithful ones.

Psalm 116:15

He will swallow up death forever.
The Almighty Lord will wipe away tears from
every face,
and he will remove the disgrace of his people
from the whole earth.
The Lord has spoken.

Isaiah 25:8

He will give light to those who live in the dark
and in death's shadow.
He will guide us into the way of peace.

Luke 1:79

Now you're in a painful situation. But I will see you again. Then you will be happy, and no one will take that happiness away from you.

John 16:22

Now you have been freed from sin and have become God's slaves. This results in a holy life and, finally, in everlasting life. The payment for sin is death, but the gift that God freely gives is everlasting life found in Christ Jesus our Lord.

Romans 6:22–23

I am convinced that nothing can ever separate us from God's love which Christ Jesus our Lord shows us. We can't be separated by death or life, by angels or rulers, by anything in the present or anything in the future, by forces or powers in the world above or in the world below, or by anything else in creation.

Romans 8:38–39

I passed on to you the most important points of doctrine that I had received: Christ died to take away our sins as the Scriptures predicted. He was placed in a tomb. He was brought back to life on the third day as the Scriptures predicted. He appeared to Cephas. Next he appeared to the twelve apostles. Then he appeared to more than 500 believers at one time. (Most of these people are still living, but some have died.) Next he appeared to James. Then he appeared to all the apostles. Last of all, he also appeared to me.

1 Corinthians 15:3–8

Christ must rule until God has put every enemy under his control. The last enemy he will destroy is death.

1 Corinthians 15:25–26

Since all of these sons and daughters have flesh and blood, Jesus took on flesh and blood to be like them. He did this so that by dying he would destroy the one who had power over death (that is, the devil). In this way he would free those who were slaves all their lives because they were afraid of dying. So Jesus helps Abraham's descendants rather than helping angels. Therefore, he had to become like his brothers and sisters so that he could be merciful. He became like them so that he could serve as a faithful chief priest in God's presence and make peace with God for their sins. Because Jesus experienced temptation when he suffered, he is able to help others when they are tempted.

Hebrews 2:14–18

Although Jesus was the Son of God, he learned to be obedient through his sufferings. After he had finished his work, he became the source of eternal salvation for everyone who obeys him.

Hebrews 5:8–9

Don't be afraid of what you are going to suffer. The devil is going to throw some of you into prison so that you may be tested. Your suffering will go on for ten days. Be faithful until death, and I will give you the crown of life.

Revelation 2:10

Depression

The LORD is near to those whose hearts are
 humble.
He saves those whose spirits are crushed.

Psalm 34:18

I waited patiently for the LORD.
 He turned to me and heard my cry for help.
 He pulled me out of a horrible pit,
  out of the mud and clay.
 He set my feet on a rock
  and made my steps secure.
 He placed a new song in my mouth,
  a song of praise to our God.
   Many will see this and worship.
   They will trust the LORD.

Psalm 40:1–3

Morning, noon, and night I complain and groan,
    and he listens to my voice.
With his peace, he will rescue my soul
    from the war waged against me,
        because there are many soldiers fighting
            against me.

Psalm 55:17–18

He will give light to those who live in the dark
    and in death's shadow.
He will guide us into the way of peace.

Luke 1:79

At the same time the Spirit also helps us in our weakness, because we don't know how to pray for what we need. But the Spirit intercedes along with our groans that cannot be expressed in words. The one who searches our hearts knows what the Spirit has in mind. The Spirit intercedes for God's people the way God wants him to.

Romans 8:26–27

Failure

The LORD is merciful, compassionate, patient,
   and always ready to forgive.

Psalm 145:8

Tear your hearts, not your clothes.
   Return to the LORD your God.
      He is merciful and compassionate,
         patient, and always ready to forgive
            and to change his plans about disaster.

Joel 2:13

Whenever you pray, forgive anything you have against
anyone. Then your Father in heaven will forgive your
failures.

Mark 11:25

The Pharisees and their scribes complained to Jesus' disciples. They asked, "Why do you eat and drink with tax collectors and sinners?" Jesus answered them, "Healthy people don't need a doctor; those who are sick do. I've come to call sinners to change the way they think and act, not to call people who think they have God's approval."

Luke 5:30–31

Jesus, our Lord, was handed over to death because of our failures and was brought back to life so that we could receive God's approval.

Romans 4:25

God's choice does not depend on a person's desire or effort, but on God's mercy.

Romans 9:16

Through the blood of his Son, we are set free from our sins. God forgives our failures because of his overflowing kindness. He poured out his kindness by giving us every kind of wisdom and insight when he revealed the mystery of his plan to us. He had decided to do this through Christ.

Ephesians 1:7–9

We were dead because of our failures, but he made us alive together with Christ. (It is God's kindness that saved you.) God has brought us back to life together with Christ Jesus and has given us a position in heaven with him. He did this through Christ Jesus out of his generosity to us in order to show his extremely rich kindness in the world to come.

Ephesians 2:5–7

Be kind to each other, sympathetic, forgiving each other as God has forgiven you through Christ.

Ephesians 4:32

You were once dead because of your failures and your uncircumcised corrupt nature. But God made you alive with Christ when he forgave all our failures.

Colossians 2:13

This is a statement that can be trusted and deserves complete acceptance: Christ Jesus came into the world to save sinners, and I am the foremost sinner.

1 Timothy 1:15

God saved us and called us to be holy, not because of what we had done, but because of his own plan and kindness. Before the world began, God planned that Christ Jesus would show us God's kindness.

2 Timothy 1:9

Persecution

With you we can walk over our enemies.
With your name we can trample those who
    attack us.

Psalm 44:5

Then my enemies will retreat when I call to you.
This I know: God is on my side.

Psalm 56:9

Even though I walk into the middle of trouble,
    you guard my life against the anger of my
        enemies.
You stretch out your hand,
    and your right hand saves me.

Psalm 138:7

Blessed are those who are persecuted for doing
    what God approves of.
    The kingdom of heaven belongs to them.
Blessed are you when people insult you,
    persecute you,

lie, and say all kinds of evil things about you
because of me.
Rejoice and be glad because you have a great reward in heaven!
The prophets who lived before you were persecuted in these ways.

Matthew 5:10–12

Jesus said, "I can guarantee this truth: Anyone who gave
up his home, brothers, sisters, mother, father, children,
or fields because of me and the Good News will certainly
receive a hundred times as much here in this life. They
will certainly receive homes, brothers, sisters, mothers,
children and fields, along with persecutions. But in the
world to come they will receive eternal life. But many
who are first will be last, and the last will be first."

Mark 10:29–31

He promised to save us from our enemies
and from the power of all who hate us.

Luke 1:71

He promised to rescue us from our enemies'
power
so that we could serve him without fear
by being holy and honorable as long as we
live.

Luke 1:74–75

What can we say about all of this? If God is for us, who can be against us? God didn't spare his own Son but handed him over to death for all of us. So he will also give us everything along with him. Who will accuse those whom God has chosen? God has approved of them. Who will condemn them? Christ has died, and more importantly, he was brought back to life. Christ has the highest position in heaven. Christ also intercedes for us. What will separate us from the love Christ has for us? Can trouble, distress, persecution, hunger, nakedness, danger, or violent death separate us from his love? As Scripture says:

> "We are being killed all day long because of you. We are thought of as sheep to be slaughtered."

The one who loves us gives us an overwhelming victory in all these difficulties. I am convinced that nothing can ever separate us from God's love which Christ Jesus our Lord shows us. We can't be separated by death or life, by angels or rulers, by anything in the present or anything in the future, by forces or powers in the world above or in the world below, or by anything else in creation.

Romans 8:31–39

In every way we're troubled, but we aren't crushed by our troubles. We're frustrated, but we don't give up. We're persecuted, but we're not abandoned. We're captured, but we're not killed.

2 Corinthians 4:8–9

Therefore, to keep me from becoming conceited, I am forced to deal with a recurring problem. That problem, Satan's messenger, torments me to keep me from being conceited. I begged the Lord three times to take it away from me. But he told me: "My kindness is all you need. My power is strongest when you are weak." So I will brag even more about my weaknesses in order that Christ's power will live in me. Therefore, I accept weakness, mistreatment, hardship, persecution, and difficulties suffered for Christ. It's clear that when I'm weak, I'm strong.

2 Corinthians 12:7–10

But the Lord is faithful and will strengthen you and protect you against the evil one.

2 Thessalonians 3:3

Don't be afraid of what you are going to suffer. The devil is going to throw some of you into prison so that you may be tested. Your suffering will go on for ten days. Be faithful until death, and I will give you the crown of life.

Revelation 2:10

Rejection

Whoever does what God wants is my brother and sister and mother.

Mark 3:35

My sheep respond to my voice, and I know who they are. They follow me, and I give them eternal life. They will never be lost, and no one will tear them away from me. My Father, who gave them to me, is greater than everyone else, and no one can tear them away from my Father.

John 10:27–29

Since Christ's blood has now given us God's approval, we are even more certain that Christ will save us from God's anger.

Romans 5:9

It is certain that death ruled because of one person's failure. It's even more certain that those who receive God's overflowing kindness and the gift of his approval will rule in life because of one person, Jesus Christ.

Romans 5:17

As sin ruled by bringing death, God's kindness would rule by bringing us his approval. This results in our living forever because of Jesus Christ our Lord.

Romans 5:21

This is true because he already knew his people and had already appointed them to have the same form as the image of his Son. Therefore, his Son is the firstborn among many children. He also called those whom he had already appointed. He approved of those whom he had called, and he gave glory to those whom he had approved of.

Romans 8:29–30

Those who are not my people
  I will call my people.
Those who are not loved
  I will call my loved ones.
Wherever they were told,
   "You are not my people,"
    they will be called children of the living God.

Romans 9:25–26

You belong to Christ, and Christ belongs to God.

1 Corinthians 3:23

God had Christ, who was sinless, take our sin so that we might receive God's approval through him.

2 Corinthians 5:21

But when the right time came, God sent his Son into the world. A woman gave birth to him, and he came under the control of God's laws. God sent him to pay for the freedom of those who were controlled by these laws so that we would be adopted as his children. Because you are God's children, God has sent the Spirit of his Son into us to call out, "Abba! Father!" So you are no longer slaves but God's children. Since you are God's children, God has also made you heirs.

Galatians 4:4–7

His favor is with everyone who has an undying love for our Lord Jesus Christ.

Ephesians 6:24

I'm convinced that God, who began this good work in you, will carry it through to completion on the day of Christ Jesus.

Philippians 1:6

But now Christ has brought you back to God by dying in his physical body. He did this so that you could come into God's presence without sin, fault, or blame.

Colossians 1:22

As a result, God in his kindness has given us his approval and we have become heirs who have the confidence that we have everlasting life.

Titus 3:7

Endure your discipline. God corrects you as a father corrects his children. All children are disciplined by their fathers.

Hebrews 12:7

Now, dear children, live in Christ. Then, when he appears we will have confidence, and when he comes we won't turn from him in shame. If you know that Christ has God's approval, you also know that everyone who does what God approves of has been born from God.

1 John 2:28–29

Consider this: The Father has given us his love. He loves us so much that we are actually called God's dear children. And that's what we are. For this reason the world doesn't recognize us, and it didn't recognize him either. Dear friends, now we are God's children. What we will be isn't completely clear yet. We do know that when Christ appears we will be like him because we will see him as he is.

1 John 3:1–2

Everyone who wins the victory this way will wear white clothes. I will never erase their names from the Book of Life. I will acknowledge them in the presence of my Father and his angels. Let the person who has ears listen to what the Spirit says to the churches.

Revelation 3:5

Look, I'm standing at the door and knocking. If anyone listens to my voice and opens the door, I'll come in and we'll eat together.

Revelation 3:20

I will allow everyone who wins the victory to sit with me on my throne, as I have won the victory and have sat down with my Father on his throne. Let the person who has ears listen to what the Spirit says to the churches.

Revelation 3:21

He said to me, "It has happened! I am the A and the Z, the beginning and the end. I will give a drink from the fountain filled with the water of life to anyone who is thirsty. It won't cost anything. Everyone who wins the victory will inherit these things. I will be their God, and they will be my children."

Revelation 21:6–7

Sickness

My body and mind may waste away,
　　but God remains the foundation of my life
　　and my inheritance forever.

Psalm 73:26

Even when you're old, I'll take care of you.
　　Even when your hair turns gray, I'll support
　　　　you.
I made you and will continue to care for you.
I'll support you and save you.

Isaiah 46:4

If any of you are having trouble, pray. If you are happy,
sing psalms. If you are sick, call for the church leaders.
Have them pray for you and anoint you with olive oil
in the name of the Lord. (Prayers offered in faith will
save those who are sick, and the Lord will cure them.)
If you have sinned, you will be forgiven. So admit your
sins to each other, and pray for each other so that you
will be healed.

James 5:13–16

Blessed is the one who has concern for helpless
people.
The LORD will rescue him in times of trouble.
The LORD will protect him and keep him alive.
He will be blessed in the land.
Do not place him at the mercy of his
enemies.
The LORD will support him on his sickbed.
You will restore this person to health when
he is ill.

Psalm 41:1–3

Sin

Purify me from sin with hyssop, and I will be
   clean.
Wash me, and I will be whiter than snow.

Psalm 51:7

How can a young person keep his life pure?
   He can do it by holding on to your word.
I wholeheartedly searched for you.
   Do not let me wander away from your
      commandments.
I have treasured your promise in my heart
   so that I may not sin against you.

Psalm 119:9–11

O Israel, put your hope in the LORD,
   because with the LORD there is mercy
      and with him there is unlimited forgiveness.
      He will rescue Israel from all its sins.

Psalm 130:7–8

"Come on now, let's discuss this!" says the LORD.
"Though your sins are bright red,
    they will become as white as snow.
Though they are dark red,
    they will become as white as wool."

Isaiah 1:18

"But this is the promise that I will make to Israel after those days," declares the LORD: "I will put my teachings inside them, and I will write those teachings on their hearts. I will be their God, and they will be my people. No longer will each person teach his neighbors or his relatives by saying, 'Know the LORD.' All of them, from the least important to the most important, will know me," declares the LORD, "because I will forgive their wickedness and I will no longer hold their sins against them."

Jeremiah 31:33–34

Who is a God like you?
    You forgive sin
        and overlook the rebellion of your faithful
            people.
    You will not be angry forever,
        because you would rather show mercy.
    You will again have compassion on us.
    You will overcome our wrongdoing.
    You will throw all our sins into the deep sea.

Micah 7:18–19

While they were eating, Jesus took bread and blessed it. He broke the bread, gave it to his disciples, and said, "Take this, and eat it. This is my body." Then he took a cup and spoke a prayer of thanksgiving. He gave it to them and said, "Drink from it, all of you. This is my blood, the blood of the promise. It is poured out for many people so that sins are forgiven."

Matthew 26:26–28

Peter answered them, "All of you must turn to God and change the way you think and act, and each of you must be baptized in the name of Jesus Christ so that your sins will be forgiven. Then you will receive the Holy Spirit as a gift. This promise belongs to you and to your children and to everyone who is far away. It belongs to everyone who worships the Lord our God."

Acts 2:38–39

There is no difference between people. Because all people have sinned, they have fallen short of God's glory. They receive God's approval freely by an act of his kindness through the price Christ Jesus paid to set us free from sin. God showed that Christ is the throne of mercy where God's approval is given through faith in Christ's blood. In his patience God waited to deal with sins committed in the past. He waited so that he could display his approval at the present time. This shows that he is a God of justice, a God who approves of people who believe in Jesus.

Romans 3:22–26

As sin ruled by bringing death, God's kindness would rule by bringing us his approval. This results in our living forever because of Jesus Christ our Lord.

Romans 5:21

So consider yourselves dead to sin's power but living for God in the power Christ Jesus gives you.

Romans 6:11

Now you have been freed from sin and have become God's slaves. This results in a holy life and, finally, in everlasting life. The payment for sin is death, but the gift that God freely gives is everlasting life found in Christ Jesus our Lord.

Romans 6:22–23

I thank God that our Lord Jesus Christ rescues me! So I am obedient to God's standards with my mind, but I am obedient to sin's standards with my corrupt nature.

Romans 7:25

So those who are believers in Christ Jesus can no longer be condemned. The standards of the Spirit, who gives life through Christ Jesus, have set you free from the standards of sin and death.

Romans 8:1–2

Sin gives death its sting, and God's standards give sin its power. Thank God that he gives us the victory through our Lord Jesus Christ.

1 Corinthians 15:56–57

God had Christ, who was sinless, take our sin so that we might receive God's approval through him.

2 Corinthians 5:21

I have been crucified with Christ. I no longer live, but Christ lives in me. The life I now live I live by believing in God's Son, who loved me and took the punishment for my sins.

Galatians 2:19–20

But Scripture states that the whole world is controlled by the power of sin. Therefore, a promise based on faith in Jesus Christ could be given to those who believe.

Galatians 3:22

Through the blood of his Son, we are set free from our sins. God forgives our failures because of his overflowing kindness. He poured out his kindness by giving us every kind of wisdom and insight when he revealed the mystery of his plan to us. He had decided to do this through Christ.

Ephesians 1:7–9

We were dead because of our failures, but he made us alive together with Christ. (It is God's kindness that saved you.) God has brought us back to life together with Christ Jesus and has given us a position in heaven with him. He did this through Christ Jesus out of his generosity to us in order to show his extremely rich kindness in the world to come.

Ephesians 2:5–7

Don't give God's Holy Spirit any reason to be upset with you. He has put his seal on you for the day you will be set free from the world of sin.

Ephesians 4:30

God has rescued us from the power of darkness and has brought us into the kingdom of his Son, whom he loves. His Son paid the price to free us, which means that our sins are forgiven.

Colossians 1:13–14

But now Christ has brought you back to God by dying in his physical body. He did this so that you could come into God's presence without sin, fault, or blame.

Colossians 1:22

He gave himself for us to set us free from every sin and to cleanse us so that we can be his special people who are enthusiastic about doing good things.

Titus 2:14

Since all of these sons and daughters have flesh and blood, Jesus took on flesh and blood to be like them. He did this so that by dying he would destroy the one who had power over death (that is, the devil). In this way he would free those who were slaves all their lives because they were afraid of dying. So Jesus helps Abraham's descendants rather than helping angels. Therefore, he had to become like his brothers and sisters so that he could be merciful. He became like them so that he could serve as a faithful chief priest in God's presence and make peace with God for their sins. Because Jesus experienced temptation when he suffered, he is able to help others when they are tempted.

Hebrews 2:14–18

Because Christ offered himself to God, he is able to bring a new promise from God. Through his death he paid the price to set people free from the sins they committed under the first promise. He did this so that those who are called can be guaranteed an inheritance that will last forever.

Hebrews 9:15

But now, at the end of the ages, he has appeared once to remove sin by his sacrifice. People die once, and after that they are judged. Likewise, Christ was sacrificed once to take away the sins of humanity, and after that he will appear a second time. This time he will not deal with sin, but he will save those who eagerly wait for him.

Hebrews 9:26–28

If any of you are having trouble, pray. If you are happy, sing psalms. If you are sick, call for the church leaders. Have them pray for you and anoint you with olive oil in the name of the Lord. (Prayers offered in faith will save those who are sick, and the Lord will cure them.) If you have sinned, you will be forgiven. So admit your sins to each other, and pray for each other so that you will be healed.

James 5:13–16

Christ carried our sins in his body on the cross so that freed from our sins, we could live a life that has God's approval. His wounds have healed you. You were like lost sheep. Now you have come back to the shepherd and bishop of your lives.

1 Peter 2:24–25

Above all, love each other warmly, because love covers many sins.

1 Peter 4:8

But if we live in the light in the same way that God is in the light, we have a relationship with each other. And the blood of his Son Jesus cleanses us from every sin.

1 John 1:7

God is faithful and reliable. If we confess our sins, he forgives them and cleanses us from everything we've done wrong.

1 John 1:9

My dear children, I'm writing this to you so that you will not sin. Yet, if anyone does sin, we have Jesus Christ, who has God's full approval. He speaks on our behalf when we come into the presence of the Father. He is the payment for our sins, and not only for our sins, but also for the sins of the whole world.

1 John 2:1–2

God has shown us his love by sending his only Son into the world so that we could have life through him. This is love: not that we have loved God, but that he loved us and sent his Son to be the payment for our sins.

1 John 4:9–10

We know that those who have been born from God don't go on sinning. Rather, the Son of God protects them, and the evil one can't harm them.

1 John 5:18

Suffering

"Because oppressed people are robbed and needy
    people groan,
  I will now arise," says the LORD.
  "I will provide safety for those who long for it."
The promises of the LORD are pure,
  like silver refined in a furnace.

                                          Psalm 12:5–6

Blessed is the one who has concern for helpless
    people.
  The LORD will rescue him in times of trouble.
  The LORD will protect him and keep him alive.
    He will be blessed in the land.
      Do not place him at the mercy of his
        enemies.
  The LORD will support him on his sickbed.
    You will restore this person to health when
      he is ill.

                                          Psalm 41:1–3

My body and mind may waste away,
 but God remains the foundation of my life
  and my inheritance forever.

Psalm 73:26

Even if he makes us suffer,
 he will have compassion
  in keeping with the richness of his mercy.

Lamentations 3:32

I will set your captives free from the waterless pit
 because of the blood that sealed my promise to
  you.
Return to your fortress, you captives who have
  hope.
 Today I tell you that I will return to you double
  blessings.

Zechariah 9:11–12

But that's not all. We also brag when we are suffering. We know that suffering creates endurance, endurance creates character, and character creates confidence. We're not ashamed to have this confidence, because God's love has been poured into our hearts by the Holy Spirit, who has been given to us.

Romans 5:3–5

God's purpose was that the body should not be divided but rather that all of its parts should feel the same concern for each other. If one part of the body suffers, all the other parts share its suffering. If one part is praised, all the others share in its happiness. You are Christ's body and each of you is an individual part of it.

1 Corinthians 12:25–27

Praise the God and Father of our Lord Jesus Christ! He is the Father who is compassionate and the God who gives comfort. He comforts us whenever we suffer. That is why whenever other people suffer, we are able to comfort them by using the same comfort we have received from God. Because Christ suffered so much for us, we can receive so much comfort from him.

2 Corinthians 1:3–5

Our suffering is light and temporary and is producing for us an eternal glory that is greater than anything we can imagine.

2 Corinthians 4:17

Therefore, to keep me from becoming conceited, I am forced to deal with a recurring problem. That problem, Satan's messenger, torments me to keep me from being conceited. I begged the Lord three times to take it away from me. But he told me: "My kindness is all you need. My power is strongest when you are weak." So I will brag even more about my weaknesses in order that Christ's power will live in me. Therefore, I accept weakness, mistreatment, hardship, persecution, and difficulties suffered for Christ. It's clear that when I'm weak, I'm strong.

2 Corinthians 12:7−10

Faith knows the power that his coming back to life gives and what it means to share his suffering. In this way I'm becoming like him in his death, with the confidence that I'll come back to life from the dead.

Philippians 3:10−11

God is the one for whom and through whom everything exists. Therefore, while God was bringing many sons and daughters to glory, it was the right time to bring Jesus, the source of their salvation, to the end of his work through suffering.

Hebrews 2:10

We need to hold on to our declaration of faith: We have a superior chief priest who has gone through the heavens. That person is Jesus, the Son of God. We have a chief priest who is able to sympathize with our weaknesses. He was tempted in every way that we are, but he didn't sin. So we can go confidently to the throne of God's kindness to receive mercy and find kindness, which will help us at the right time.

Hebrews 4:14−16

Although Jesus was the Son of God, he learned to be obedient through his sufferings. After he had finished his work, he became the source of eternal salvation for everyone who obeys him.

Hebrews 5:8–9

My brothers and sisters, be very happy when you are tested in different ways. You know that such testing of your faith produces endurance.

James 1:2–3

But be happy as you share Christ's sufferings. Then you will also be full of joy when he appears again in his glory. If you are insulted because of the name of Christ, you are blessed because the Spirit of glory—the Spirit of God—is resting on you.

1 Peter 4:13–14

Those who suffer because that is God's will for them must entrust themselves to a faithful creator and continue to do what is good.

1 Peter 4:19

Keep your mind clear, and be alert. Your opponent the devil is prowling around like a roaring lion as he looks for someone to devour. Be firm in the faith and resist him, knowing that other believers throughout the world are going through the same kind of suffering. God, who shows you his kindness and who has called you through Christ Jesus to his eternal glory, will restore you, strengthen you, make you strong, and support you as you suffer for a little while.

1 Peter 5:8–10

Don't be afraid of what you are going to suffer. The devil is going to throw some of you into prison so that you may be tested. Your suffering will go on for ten days. Be faithful until death, and I will give you the crown of life.

Revelation 2:10

Temptation

How can a young person keep his life pure?
　　He can do it by holding on to your word.
I wholeheartedly searched for you.
　　Do not let me wander away from your
　　　　commandments.
I have treasured your promise in my heart
　　so that I may not sin against you.

Psalm 119:9–11

I thank God that our Lord Jesus Christ rescues me! So I am obedient to God's standards with my mind, but I am obedient to sin's standards with my corrupt nature.

Romans 7:25

There isn't any temptation that you have experienced which is unusual for humans. God, who faithfully keeps his promises, will not allow you to be tempted beyond your power to resist. But when you are tempted, he will also give you the ability to endure the temptation as your way of escape.

1 Corinthians 10:13

The weapons we use in our fight are not made by humans. Rather, they are powerful weapons from God. With them we destroy people's defenses, that is, their arguments and all their intellectual arrogance that oppose the knowledge of God. We take every thought captive so that it is obedient to Christ.

2 Corinthians 10:4–5

Finally, receive your power from the Lord and from his mighty strength. Put on all the armor that God supplies. In this way you can take a stand against the devil's strategies. This is not a wrestling match against a human opponent. We are wrestling with rulers, authorities, the powers who govern this world of darkness, and spiritual forces that control evil in the heavenly world. For this reason, take up all the armor that God supplies. Then you will be able to take a stand during these evil days. Once you have overcome all obstacles, you will be able to stand your ground.

Ephesians 6:10–13

God has rescued us from the power of darkness and has brought us into the kingdom of his Son, whom he loves. His Son paid the price to free us, which means that our sins are forgiven.

Colossians 1:13–14

But the Lord is faithful and will strengthen you and protect you against the evil one.

2 Thessalonians 3:3

Since all of these sons and daughters have flesh and blood, Jesus took on flesh and blood to be like them. He did this so that by dying he would destroy the one who had power over death (that is, the devil). In this way he would free those who were slaves all their lives because they were afraid of dying. So Jesus helps Abraham's descendants rather than helping angels. Therefore, he had to become like his brothers and sisters so that he could be merciful. He became like them so that he could serve as a faithful chief priest in God's presence and make peace with God for their sins. Because Jesus experienced temptation when he suffered, he is able to help others when they are tempted.

Hebrews 2:14–18

We need to hold on to our declaration of faith: We have a superior chief priest who has gone through the heavens. That person is Jesus, the Son of God. We have a chief priest who is able to sympathize with our weaknesses. He was tempted in every way that we are, but he didn't sin. So we can go confidently to the throne of God's kindness to receive mercy and find kindness, which will help us at the right time.

Hebrews 4:14–16

Keep your mind clear, and be alert. Your opponent the devil is prowling around like a roaring lion as he looks for someone to devour. Be firm in the faith and resist him, knowing that other believers throughout the world are going through the same kind of suffering. God, who shows you his kindness and who has called you through Christ Jesus to his eternal glory, will restore you, strengthen you, make you strong, and support you as you suffer for a little while.

1 Peter 5:8–10

Since the Lord did all this, he knows how to rescue godly people when they are tested. He also knows how to hold immoral people for punishment on the day of judgment.

2 Peter 2:9

People can know our Lord and Savior Jesus Christ and escape the world's filth.

2 Peter 2:20

Through God's Promises
I Experience . . .

Eternal Life

Certainly, goodness and mercy will stay close to
    me all the days of my life,
  and I will remain in the LORD's house for days
    without end.

Psalm 23:6

This God is our God forever and ever.
  He will lead us beyond death.

Psalm 48:14

I will create a new heaven and a new earth.
  Past things will not be remembered.
  They will not come to mind.

Isaiah 65:17

Jesus said, "I can guarantee this truth: Anyone who gave up his home, brothers, sisters, mother, father, children, or fields because of me and the Good News will certainly receive a hundred times as much here in this life. They will certainly receive homes, brothers, sisters, mothers, children and fields, along with persecutions. But in the world to come they will receive eternal life. But many who are first will be last, and the last will be first."

Mark 10:29–31

Christ means everything to me in this life, and when I die I'll have even more.

Philippians 1:21

This is a statement that can be trusted:
    If we have died with him, we will live with him.
    If we endure, we will rule with him.
    If we disown him, he will disown us.
    If we are unfaithful, he remains faithful
        because he cannot be untrue to himself.

2 Timothy 2:11–13

Let the person who has ears listen to what the Spirit says to the churches. I will give the privilege of eating from the tree of life, which stands in the paradise of God, to everyone who wins the victory.

Revelation 2:7

Don't be afraid of what you are going to suffer. The devil is going to throw some of you into prison so that you may be tested. Your suffering will go on for ten days. Be faithful until death, and I will give you the crown of life.

Revelation 2:10

I will make everyone who wins the victory a pillar in the temple of my God. They will never leave it again. I will write on them the name of my God, the name of the city of my God (the New Jerusalem coming down out of heaven from my God), and my new name.

Revelation 3:12

I heard a voice from heaven saying, "Write this: From now on those who die believing in the Lord are blessed."

Revelation 14:13

I saw a new heaven and a new earth, because the first heaven and earth had disappeared, and the sea was gone. Then I saw the holy city, New Jerusalem, coming down from God out of heaven, dressed like a bride ready for her husband. I heard a loud voice from the throne say, "God lives with humans! God will make his home with them, and they will be his people. God himself will be with them and be their God. He will wipe every tear from their eyes. There won't be any more death. There won't be any grief, crying, or pain, because the first things have disappeared."

Revelation 21:1–4

Gifts from God

God said, "I have given you every plant with seeds on the face of the earth and every tree that has fruit with seeds. This will be your food. I have given all green plants as food to every land animal, every bird in the sky, and every animal that crawls on the earth—every living, breathing animal." And so it was.

Genesis 1:29–30

The LORD is my inheritance and my cup.
   You are the one who determines my destiny.
   Your boundary lines mark out pleasant places
      for me.
Indeed, my inheritance is something beautiful.

Psalm 16:5–6

God arms me with strength
   and makes my way perfect.

Psalm 18:32

The LORD is my strength and my shield.
My heart trusted him, so I received help.
My heart is triumphant; I give thanks to him with
my song.

Psalm 28:7

The LORD will give power to his people.
The LORD will bless his people with peace.

Psalm 29:11

O God, you have heard my vows.
You have given me the inheritance
that belongs to those who fear your name.

Psalm 61:5

You crown the year with your goodness,
and richness overflows wherever you are.
The pastures in the desert overflow with
richness.
The hills are surrounded with joy.

Psalm 65:11–12

God, the God of Israel, is awe-inspiring in his
holy place.
He gives strength and power to his people.
Thanks be to God!

Psalm 68:35

My body and mind may waste away,
   but God remains the foundation of my life
      and my inheritance forever.

Psalm 73:26

The Lord God is a sun and shield.
The Lord grants favor and honor.
He does not hold back any blessing
   from those who live innocently.

Psalm 84:11

You said, "I have made a promise to my chosen
      one.
I swore this oath to my servant David:
   'I will make your dynasty continue forever.
   I built your throne to last throughout every
      generation.'"

Psalm 89:3–4

O Lord, blessed is the person
   whom you discipline and instruct from your
      teachings.
      You give him peace and quiet from times of
         trouble
      while a pit is dug to trap wicked people.

Psalm 94:12–13

But from everlasting to everlasting,
  the LORD's mercy is on those who fear him.
    His righteousness belongs
      to their children and grandchildren.

Psalm 103:17

He provides food for those who fear him.
He always remembers his promise.

Psalm 111:5

Children are an inheritance from the LORD.
  They are a reward from him.
    The children born to a man when he is young
      are like arrows in the hand of a warrior.
        Blessed is the man who has filled his
          quiver with them.
        He will not be put to shame
          when he speaks with his enemies in
            the city gate.

Psalm 127:3–5

The LORD swore an oath to David.
  This is a truth he will not take back:
    "I will set one of your own descendants on
      your throne.
    If your sons are faithful to my promise
      and my written instructions that I will
        teach them,
    then their descendants will also sit on your
      throne forever."

Psalm 132:11–12

There I will make a horn sprout up for David.
  I will prepare a lamp for my anointed one.
  I will clothe his enemies with shame,
    but the crown on my anointed one will shine.

Psalm 132:17–18

He gives food to every living creature—
  because his mercy endures forever.

Psalm 136:25

He brings about justice for those who are
    oppressed.
  He gives food to those who are hungry.
The LORD sets prisoners free.

Psalm 146:7

The LORD gives wisdom.
  From his mouth come knowledge and
      understanding.
    He has reserved priceless wisdom for decent
        people.
He is a shield for those who walk in integrity
  in order to guard those on paths of justice
    and to watch over the way of his godly ones.

Proverbs 2:6–8

On the heels of humility (the fear of the LORD)
  are riches and honor and life.

Proverbs 22:4

He gives strength to those who grow tired
    and increases the strength of those who are
        weak.
Even young people grow tired and become weary,
    and young men will stumble and fall.
Yet, the strength of those who wait with hope in
    the Lord
will be renewed.
        They will soar on wings like eagles.
            They will run and won't become weary.
            They will walk and won't grow tired.

Isaiah 40:29–31

"This is my promise to them," says the Lord. "My Spirit, who is on you, and my words that I put in your mouth will not leave you. They will be with your children and your grandchildren permanently," says the Lord.

Isaiah 59:21

"But this is the promise that I will make to Israel after those days," declares the Lord: "I will put my teachings inside them, and I will write those teachings on their hearts. I will be their God, and they will be my people. No longer will each person teach his neighbors or his relatives by saying, 'Know the Lord.' All of them, from the least important to the most important, will know me," declares the Lord, "because I will forgive their wickedness and I will no longer hold their sins against them."

Jeremiah 31:33–34

He will give light to those who live in the dark
    and in death's shadow.
He will guide us into the way of peace.

Luke 1:79

Don't be afraid, little flock. Your Father is pleased to give you the kingdom.

Luke 12:32

Each of us has received one gift after another because of all that the Word is.

John 1:16

A thief comes to steal, kill, and destroy. But I came so that my sheep will have life and so that they will have everything they need.

John 10:10

I will ask the Father, and he will give you another helper who will be with you forever. That helper is the Spirit of Truth. The world cannot accept him, because it doesn't see or know him. You know him, because he lives with you and will be in you.

John 14:16–17

So it was not by obeying Moses' Teachings that Abraham or his descendants received the promise that he would inherit the world. Rather, it was through God's approval of his faith.

Romans 4:13

Now that we have God's approval by faith, we have peace with God because of what our Lord Jesus Christ has done. Through Christ we can approach God and stand in his favor. So we brag because of our confidence that we will receive glory from God.

Romans 5:1–2

Since Christ's blood has now given us God's approval, we are even more certain that Christ will save us from God's anger.

Romans 5:9

So consider yourselves dead to sin's power but living for God in the power Christ Jesus gives you.

Romans 6:11

Now you have been freed from sin and have become God's slaves. This results in a holy life and, finally, in everlasting life. The payment for sin is death, but the gift that God freely gives is everlasting life found in Christ Jesus our Lord.

Romans 6:22–23

So those who are believers in Christ Jesus can no longer be condemned. The standards of the Spirit, who gives life through Christ Jesus, have set you free from the standards of sin and death.

Romans 8:1–2

This is true because he already knew his people and had already appointed them to have the same form as the image of his Son. Therefore, his Son is the firstborn among many children. He also called those whom he had already appointed. He approved of those whom he had called, and he gave glory to those whom he had approved of.

Romans 8:29–30

God in his kindness gave each of us different gifts. If your gift is speaking God's word, make sure what you say agrees with the Christian faith. If your gift is serving, then devote yourself to serving. If it is teaching, devote yourself to teaching. If it is encouraging others, devote yourself to giving encouragement. If it is sharing, be generous. If it is leadership, lead enthusiastically. If it is helping people in need, help them cheerfully.

Romans 12:6–8

He will continue to give you strength until the end so that no one can accuse you of anything on the day of our Lord Jesus Christ. God faithfully keeps his promises. He called you to be partners with his Son Jesus Christ our Lord.

1 Corinthians 1:8–9

Now, we didn't receive the spirit that belongs to the world. Instead, we received the Spirit who comes from God so that we could know the things which God has freely given us.

1 Corinthians 2:12

There isn't any temptation that you have experienced which is unusual for humans. God, who faithfully keeps his promises, will not allow you to be tempted beyond your power to resist. But when you are tempted, he will also give you the ability to endure the temptation as your way of escape.

1 Corinthians 10:13

There are different spiritual gifts, but the same Spirit gives them. There are different ways of serving, and yet the same Lord is served. There are different types of work to do, but the same God produces every gift in every person.

1 Corinthians 12:4–6

Christ gives us confidence about you in God's presence. By ourselves we are not qualified in any way to claim that we can do anything. Rather, God makes us qualified. He has also qualified us to be ministers of a new promise, a spiritual promise, not a written one. Clearly, what was written brings death, but the Spirit brings life.

2 Corinthians 3:4–6

Whoever is a believer in Christ is a new creation. The old way of living has disappeared. A new way of living has come into existence. God has done all this. He has restored our relationship with him through Christ, and has given us this ministry of restoring relationships.

2 Corinthians 5:17–18

You know about the kindness of our Lord Jesus Christ. He was rich, yet for your sake he became poor in order to make you rich through his poverty.

2 Corinthians 8:9

The weapons we use in our fight are not made by humans. Rather, they are powerful weapons from God. With them we destroy people's defenses, that is, their arguments and all their intellectual arrogance that oppose the knowledge of God. We take every thought captive so that it is obedient to Christ.

2 Corinthians 10:4−5

Abraham serves as an example. He believed God, and that faith was regarded by God to be his approval of Abraham. You must understand that people who have faith are Abraham's descendants. Scripture saw ahead of time that God would give his approval to non-Jewish people who have faith. So Scripture announced the Good News to Abraham ahead of time when it said, "Through you all the people of the world will be blessed." So people who believe are blessed together with Abraham, the man of faith.

Galatians 3:6−9

But when the right time came, God sent his Son into the world. A woman gave birth to him, and he came under the control of God's laws. God sent him to pay for the freedom of those who were controlled by these laws so that we would be adopted as his children. Because you are God's children, God has sent the Spirit of his Son into us to call out, "Abba! Father!" So you are no longer slaves but God's children. Since you are God's children, God has also made you heirs.

Galatians 4:4–7

Praise the God and Father of our Lord Jesus Christ! Through Christ, God has blessed us with every spiritual blessing that heaven has to offer.

Ephesians 1:3

Through the blood of his Son, we are set free from our sins. God forgives our failures because of his overflowing kindness. He poured out his kindness by giving us every kind of wisdom and insight when he revealed the mystery of his plan to us. He had decided to do this through Christ.

Ephesians 1:7–9

You heard and believed the message of truth, the Good News that he has saved you. In him you were sealed with the Holy Spirit whom he promised. This Holy Spirit is the guarantee that we will receive our inheritance. We have this guarantee until we are set free to belong to him. God receives praise and glory for this.

Ephesians 1:13–14

God has made us what we are. He has created us in Christ Jesus to live lives filled with good works that he has prepared for us to do.

Ephesians 2:10

I'm asking God to give you a gift from the wealth of his glory. I pray that he would give you inner strength and power through his Spirit.

Ephesians 3:16

God's favor has been given to each of us. It was measured out to us by Christ who gave it. That's why the Scriptures say:
> "When he went to the highest place,
> he took captive those who had captured us
> and gave gifts to people."

Ephesians 4:7–8

He also gave apostles, prophets, missionaries, as well as pastors and teachers as gifts to his church. Their purpose is to prepare God's people to serve and to build up the body of Christ. This is to continue until all of us are united in our faith and in our knowledge about God's Son, until we become mature, until we measure up to Christ, who is the standard.

Ephesians 4:11–13

Finally, receive your power from the Lord and from his mighty strength. Put on all the armor that God supplies. In this way you can take a stand against the devil's strategies. This is not a wrestling match against a human opponent. We are wrestling with rulers, authorities, the powers who govern this world of darkness, and spiritual forces that control evil in the heavenly world. For this reason, take up all the armor that God supplies. Then you will be able to take a stand during these evil days. Once you have overcome all obstacles, you will be able to stand your ground.

Ephesians 6:10–13

God wanted his people throughout the world to know the glorious riches of this mystery—which is Christ living in you, giving you the hope of glory.

Colossians 1:27

Slaves, always obey your earthly masters. Don't obey them only while you're being watched, as if you merely wanted to please people. Be sincere in your motives out of respect for your real master. Whatever you do, do it wholeheartedly as though you were working for your real master and not merely for humans. You know that your real master will give you an inheritance as your reward. It is Christ, your real master, whom you are serving.

Colossians 3:22–24

May the God who gives peace make you holy in every way. May he keep your whole being—spirit, soul, and body—blameless when our Lord Jesus Christ comes. The one who calls you is faithful, and he will do this.

1 Thessalonians 5:23–24

We always have to thank God for you, brothers and sisters. You are loved by the Lord and we thank God that in the beginning he chose you to be saved through a life of spiritual devotion and faith in the truth. With this in mind he called you by the Good News which we told you so that you would obtain the glory of our Lord Jesus Christ.

2 Thessalonians 2:13–14

God didn't give us a cowardly spirit but a spirit of power, love, and good judgment.

2 Timothy 1:7

After all, God's saving kindness has appeared for the benefit of all people. It trains us to avoid ungodly lives filled with worldly desires so that we can live self-controlled, moral, and godly lives in this present world.

Titus 2:11–12

He gave himself for us to set us free from every sin and to cleanse us so that we can be his special people who are enthusiastic about doing good things.

Titus 2:14

God is the one for whom and through whom everything exists. Therefore, while God was bringing many sons and daughters to glory, it was the right time to bring Jesus, the source of their salvation, to the end of his work through suffering.

Hebrews 2:10

If any of you needs wisdom to know what you should do, you should ask God, and he will give it to you. God is generous to everyone and doesn't find fault with them.

James 1:5

Don't pay people back with evil for the evil they do to you, or ridicule those who ridicule you. Instead, bless them, because you were called to inherit a blessing.

1 Peter 3:9

But be happy as you share Christ's sufferings. Then you will also be full of joy when he appears again in his glory. If you are insulted because of the name of Christ, you are blessed because the Spirit of glory—the Spirit of God—is resting on you.

1 Peter 4:13–14

God's divine power has given us everything we need for life and for godliness. This power was given to us through knowledge of the one who called us by his own glory and integrity. Through his glory and integrity he has given us his promises that are of the highest value. Through these promises you will share in the divine nature because you have escaped the corruption that sinful desires cause in the world.

2 Peter 1:3–4

First, you must understand this: No prophecy in Scripture is a matter of one's own interpretation. No prophecy ever originated from humans. Instead, it was given by the Holy Spirit as humans spoke under God's direction.

2 Peter 1:20–21

He said to me, "It has happened! I am the A and the Z, the beginning and the end. I will give a drink from the fountain filled with the water of life to anyone who is thirsty. It won't cost anything. Everyone who wins the victory will inherit these things. I will be their God, and they will be my children."

Revelation 21:6–7

Marriage as God Intended

Then the LORD God said, "It is not good for the man to be alone. I will make a helper who is right for him."

That is why a man will leave his father and mother and will be united with his wife, and they will become one flesh.

Genesis 2:18, 24

Whoever finds a wife finds something good
and has obtained favor from the LORD.

Proverbs 18:22

Husbands, love your wives as Christ loved the church and gave his life for it. He did this to make the church holy by cleansing it, washing it using water along with spoken words. Then he could present it to himself as a glorious church, without any kind of stain or wrinkle—holy and without faults.

Ephesians 5:25–27

Marriage is honorable in every way, so husbands and wives should be faithful to each other. God will judge those who commit sexual sins, especially those who commit adultery.

Hebrews 13:4

The Mercy of the Father

You gave me life and mercy.
  Your watchfulness has preserved my spirit.

  Job 10:12

But God will buy me back from the power of hell
  because he will take me.

  Psalm 49:15

Whoever offers thanks as a sacrifice honors me.
I will let everyone who continues in my way
  see the salvation that comes from God.

  Psalm 50:23

But I call on God,
  and the LORD saves me.

  Psalm 55:16

Turn your burdens over to the LORD,
  and he will take care of you.
    He will never let the righteous person
    stumble.

  Psalm 55:22

Mercy and truth have met.
Righteousness and peace have kissed.
Truth sprouts from the ground,
  and righteousness looks down from heaven.
The LORD will certainly give us what is good,
  and our land will produce crops.
Righteousness will go ahead of him
  and make a path for his steps.

Psalm 85:10–13

The LORD is compassionate, merciful, patient,
  and always ready to forgive.

Psalm 103:8

But from everlasting to everlasting,
  the LORD's mercy is on those who fear him.
    His righteousness belongs
      to their children and grandchildren,
      to those who are faithful to his promise,
      to those who remember to follow his
        guiding principles.

Psalm 103:17–18

Who is like the LORD our God?
  He is seated on his high throne.
  He bends down to look at heaven and earth.
  He lifts the poor from the dust.
  He lifts the needy from a garbage heap.
  He seats them with influential people,
    with the influential leaders of his people.

He makes a woman who is in a childless home
    a joyful mother.
Hallelujah!

Psalm 113:5–9

He will bless those who fear the LORD,
    from the least important to the most
        important.

Psalm 115:13

O Israel, put your hope in the LORD,
    because with the LORD there is mercy
        and with him there is unlimited forgiveness.
        He will rescue Israel from all its sins.

Psalm 130:7–8

The LORD is merciful, compassionate, patient,
    and always ready to forgive.

Psalm 145:8

Even if he makes us suffer,
    he will have compassion
        in keeping with the richness of his mercy.

Lamentations 3:32

Tear your hearts, not your clothes.
    Return to the LORD your God.
        He is merciful and compassionate,
            patient, and always ready to forgive
                and to change his plans about disaster.

Joel 2:13

Who is a God like you?
>You forgive sin
>>and overlook the rebellion of your faithful
>>people.
>You will not be angry forever,
>>because you would rather show mercy.
>You will again have compassion on us.
>You will overcome our wrongdoing.
>You will throw all our sins into the deep sea.

Micah 7:18–19

What do you think? Suppose a man has 100 sheep and one of them strays. Won't he leave the 99 sheep in the hills to look for the one that has strayed? I can guarantee this truth: If he finds it, he is happier about it than about the 99 that have not strayed. In the same way, your Father in heaven does not want one of these little ones to be lost.

Matthew 18:12–14

>A new day will dawn on us from above
>>because our God is loving and merciful.

Luke 1:78

God loved the world this way: He gave his only Son so that everyone who believes in him will not die but will have eternal life.

John 3:16

God sent his Son into the world, not to condemn the world, but to save the world.

John 3:17

The one who sent me doesn't want me to lose any of those he gave me. He wants me to bring them back to life on the last day.

John 6:39

Peter answered them, "All of you must turn to God and change the way you think and act, and each of you must be baptized in the name of Jesus Christ so that your sins will be forgiven. Then you will receive the Holy Spirit as a gift. This promise belongs to you and to your children and to everyone who is far away. It belongs to everyone who worships the Lord our God."

Acts 2:38–39

I'm not ashamed of the Good News. It is God's power to save everyone who believes, Jews first and Greeks as well. God's approval is revealed in this Good News. This approval begins and ends with faith as Scripture says, "The person who has God's approval will live by faith."

Romans 1:16–17

Now, the way to receive God's approval has been made plain in a way other than Moses' Teachings. Moses' Teachings and the Prophets tell us this. Everyone who believes has God's approval through faith in Jesus Christ.

Romans 3:21–22

When people work, their pay is not regarded as a gift but something they have earned. However, when people don't work but believe God, the one who approves ungodly people, their faith is regarded as God's approval.

Romans 4:4–5

It is certain that death ruled because of one person's failure. It's even more certain that those who receive God's overflowing kindness and the gift of his approval will rule in life because of one person, Jesus Christ.

Romans 5:17

God's choice does not depend on a person's desire or effort, but on God's mercy.

Romans 9:16

God had Christ, who was sinless, take our sin so that we might receive God's approval through him.

2 Corinthians 5:21

We were dead because of our failures, but he made us alive together with Christ. (It is God's kindness that saved you.) God has brought us back to life together with Christ Jesus and has given us a position in heaven with him. He did this through Christ Jesus out of his generosity to us in order to show his extremely rich kindness in the world to come. God saved you through faith as an act of kindness. You had nothing to do with it. Being saved is a gift from God. It's not the result of anything you've done, so no one can brag about it.

Ephesians 2:5–9

Good will, mercy, and peace from God the Father and Christ Jesus our Lord are yours!

1 Timothy 1:2

Certainly, we work hard and struggle to live a godly life, because we place our confidence in the living God. He is the Savior of all people, especially of those who believe.

1 Timothy 4:10

God saved us and called us to be holy, not because of what we had done, but because of his own plan and kindness. Before the world began, God planned that Christ Jesus would show us God's kindness.

2 Timothy 1:9

So we can go confidently to the throne of God's kindness to receive mercy and find kindness, which will help us at the right time.

Hebrews 4:16

The Mercy of the Son

Come to me, all who are tired from carrying heavy loads, and I will give you rest. Place my yoke over your shoulders, and learn from me, because I am gentle and humble. Then you will find rest for yourselves because my yoke is easy and my burden is light.

Matthew 11:28–30

While they were eating, Jesus took bread and blessed it. He broke the bread, gave it to his disciples, and said, "Take this, and eat it. This is my body." Then he took a cup and spoke a prayer of thanksgiving. He gave it to them and said, "Drink from it, all of you. This is my blood, the blood of the promise. It is poured out for many people so that sins are forgiven."

Matthew 26:26–28

He will give light to those who live in the dark
    and in death's shadow.
He will guide us into the way of peace.

Luke 1:79

The Pharisees and their scribes complained to Jesus' disciples. They asked, "Why do you eat and drink with tax collectors and sinners?" Jesus answered them, "Healthy people don't need a doctor; those who are sick do. I've come to call sinners to change the way they think and act, not to call people who think they have God's approval."

Luke 5:30–31

However, he gave the right to become God's children to everyone who believed in him. These people didn't become God's children in a physical way—from a human impulse or from a husband's desire to have a child. They were born from God.

John 1:12–13

There is no difference between people. Because all people have sinned, they have fallen short of God's glory. They receive God's approval freely by an act of his kindness through the price Christ Jesus paid to set us free from sin. God showed that Christ is the throne of mercy where God's approval is given through faith in Christ's blood. In his patience God waited to deal with sins committed in the past. He waited so that he could display his approval at the present time. This shows that he is a God of justice, a God who approves of people who believe in Jesus.

Romans 3:22–26

Jesus, our Lord, was handed over to death because of our failures and was brought back to life so that we could receive God's approval.

Romans 4:25

Since Christ's blood has now given us God's approval, we are even more certain that Christ will save us from God's anger.

Romans 5:9

This is a statement that can be trusted and deserves complete acceptance: Christ Jesus came into the world to save sinners, and I am the foremost sinner.

1 Timothy 1:15

Realize that you weren't set free from the worthless life handed down to you from your ancestors by a payment of silver or gold which can be destroyed. Rather, the payment that freed you was the precious blood of Christ, the lamb with no defects or imperfections.

1 Peter 1:18–19

Miracles

A child will be born for us.
   A son will be given to us.
      The government will rest on his shoulders.
   He will be named:
      Wonderful Counselor,
      Mighty God,
      Everlasting Father,
      Prince of Peace.
His government and peace will have unlimited
      growth.
   He will establish David's throne and kingdom.
   He will uphold it with justice and righ-
      teousness now and forever.
The LORD of Armies is determined to do this!

Isaiah 9:6–7

Have faith that you will receive whatever you ask for
in prayer.

Matthew 21:22

Jesus said to him, "As far as possibilities go, everything is possible for the person who believes."

Mark 9:23

Jesus said to them, "Have faith in God! I can guarantee this truth: This is what will be done for someone who doesn't doubt but believes what he says will happen: He can say to this mountain, 'Be uprooted and thrown into the sea,' and it will be done for him. That's why I tell you to have faith that you have already received whatever you pray for, and it will be yours."

Mark 11:22–24

I will do anything you ask the Father in my name so that the Father will be given glory because of the Son. If you ask me to do something, I will do it.

John 14:13–14

If you live in me and what I say lives in you, then ask for anything you want, and it will be yours. You give glory to my Father when you produce a lot of fruit and therefore show that you are my disciples.

John 15:7–8

You didn't choose me, but I chose you. I have appointed you to go, to produce fruit that will last, and to ask the Father in my name to give you whatever you ask for.

John 15:16

If any of you are having trouble, pray. If you are happy, sing psalms. If you are sick, call for the church leaders. Have them pray for you and anoint you with olive oil in the name of the Lord. (Prayers offered in faith will save those who are sick, and the Lord will cure them.) If you have sinned, you will be forgiven. So admit your sins to each other, and pray for each other so that you will be healed.

James 5:13–16

We are confident that God listens to us if we ask for anything that has his approval. We know that he listens to our requests. So we know that we already have what we ask him for.

1 John 5:14–15

Opportunities

Every path of the LORD is one of mercy and truth
for those who cling to his promise and written
instructions.

Psalm 25:10

A person's steps are directed by the LORD,
and the LORD delights in his way.
When he falls, he will not be thrown down
headfirst
because the LORD holds on to his hand.

Psalm 37:23–24

Wait with hope for the LORD, and follow his path,
and he will honor you by giving you the land.
When wicked people are cut off, you will
see it.

Psalm 37:34

You crown the year with your goodness,
  and richness overflows wherever you are.
    The pastures in the desert overflow with
      richness.
    The hills are surrounded with joy.

Psalm 65:11–12

Trust the LORD with all your heart,
  and do not rely on your own understanding.
In all your ways acknowledge him,
  and he will make your paths smooth.

Proverbs 3:5–6

Whoever gives attention to the LORD's word
  prospers,
    and blessed is the person who trusts the LORD.

Proverbs 16:20

If you give some of your own food to feed those
  who are hungry
    and to satisfy the needs of those who are
      humble,
then your light will rise in the dark,
  and your darkness will become as bright as the
    noonday sun.
The LORD will continually guide you
  and satisfy you even in sun-baked places.

He will strengthen your bones.
    You will become like a watered garden
        and like a spring whose water does not stop
            flowing.
Your people will rebuild the ancient ruins
    and restore the foundations of past
        generations.
You will be called the Rebuilder of Broken Walls
    and the Restorer of Streets Where People Live.

                                    Isaiah 58:10–12

God's Promises
Enable My . . .

Belief

Whoever gives attention to the LORD's word
   prospers,
   and blessed is the person who trusts the LORD.

Proverbs 16:20

Jesus said to him, "As far as possibilities go, everything is possible for the person who believes."

Mark 9:23

Jesus said to them, "Have faith in God! I can guarantee this truth: This is what will be done for someone who doesn't doubt but believes what he says will happen: He can say to this mountain, 'Be uprooted and thrown into the sea,' and it will be done for him. That's why I tell you to have faith that you have already received whatever you pray for, and it will be yours."

Mark 11:22–24

God loved the world this way: He gave his only Son so that everyone who believes in him will not die but will have eternal life.

John 3:16

So Jesus said to those Jews who believed in him, "If you live by what I say, you are truly my disciples. You will know the truth, and the truth will set you free."

John 8:31–32

God showed that Christ is the throne of mercy where God's approval is given through faith in Christ's blood. In his patience God waited to deal with sins committed in the past. He waited so that he could display his approval at the present time. This shows that he is a God of justice, a God who approves of people who believe in Jesus.

Romans 3:25–26

So those who are believers in Christ Jesus can no longer be condemned. The standards of the Spirit, who gives life through Christ Jesus, have set you free from the standards of sin and death.

Romans 8:1–2

Whoever is a believer in Christ is a new creation. The old way of living has disappeared. A new way of living has come into existence. God has done all this. He has restored our relationship with him through Christ, and has given us this ministry of restoring relationships.

2 Corinthians 5:17–18

Abraham serves as an example. He believed God, and that faith was regarded by God to be his approval of Abraham. You must understand that people who have faith are Abraham's descendants. Scripture saw ahead of time that God would give his approval to non-Jewish people who have faith. So Scripture announced the Good News to Abraham ahead of time when it said, "Through you all the people of the world will be blessed." So people who believe are blessed together with Abraham, the man of faith.

Galatians 3:6–9

You heard and believed the message of truth, the Good News that he has saved you. In him you were sealed with the Holy Spirit whom he promised. This Holy Spirit is the guarantee that we will receive our inheritance. We have this guarantee until we are set free to belong to him. God receives praise and glory for this.

Ephesians 1:13–14

Here is another reason why we never stop thanking God: When you received God's word from us, you realized it wasn't the word of humans. Instead, you accepted it for what it really is—the word of God. This word is at work in you believers.

1 Thessalonians 2:13

We who believe are entering that place of rest.

Hebrews 4:3

Courage

Be strong and courageous. Don't tremble! Don't be afraid of them! The LORD your God is the one who is going with you. He won't abandon you or leave you.

Deuteronomy 31:6

I have commanded you, "Be strong and courageous! Don't tremble or be terrified, because the LORD your God is with you wherever you go."

Joshua 1:9

You won't fight this battle. Instead, take your position, stand still, and see the victory of the LORD for you, Judah and Jerusalem. Don't be frightened or terrified. Tomorrow go out to face them. The LORD is with you.

2 Chronicles 20:17

Even though I walk through the dark valley of death,
because you are with me, I fear no harm.
Your rod and your staff give me courage.

Psalm 23:4

Wait with hope for the Lord.
Be strong, and let your heart be courageous.
Yes, wait with hope for the Lord.

Psalm 27:14

Do not be afraid of sudden terror
　or of the destruction of wicked people when it
　　　comes.
　　The Lord will be your confidence.
　　He will keep your foot from getting caught.

Proverbs 3:25–26

Don't be afraid, because I am with you.
Don't be intimidated; I am your God.
　I will strengthen you.

Isaiah 41:10

The High and Lofty One lives forever, and his
　　name is holy.
This is what he says:
　I live in a high and holy place.
　　But I am with those who are crushed and
　　　humble.
　　　I will renew the spirit of those who are
　　　　humble
　　　　and the courage of those who are
　　　　　crushed.

I will not accuse you forever.
I will not be angry with you forever.
  Otherwise, the spirits, the lives of those I've
    made,
    would grow faint in my presence.

Isaiah 57:15–16

Blessed is the person who trusts the LORD.
  The LORD will be his confidence.

Jeremiah 17:7

On that day Jerusalem will be told,
  "Do not be afraid, Zion!
  Do not lose courage!"
The LORD your God is with you.
  He is a hero who saves you.
    He happily rejoices over you,
      renews you with his love,
        and celebrates over you with shouts
        of joy.

Zephaniah 3:16–17

We know that all things work together for the good of those who love God—those whom he has called according to his plan.

Romans 8:28

Everything written long ago was written to teach us so that we would have confidence through the endurance and encouragement which the Scriptures give us.

Romans 15:4

I want you to know how hard I work for you, for the people of Laodicea, and for people I have never met. Because they are united in love, I work so that they may be encouraged by all the riches that come from a complete understanding of Christ. He is the mystery of God.

Colossians 2:1–2

No fear exists where his love is. Rather, perfect love gets rid of fear, because fear involves punishment. The person who lives in fear doesn't have perfect love.

1 John 4:18

Don't be afraid of what you are going to suffer. The devil is going to throw some of you into prison so that you may be tested. Your suffering will go on for ten days. Be faithful until death, and I will give you the crown of life.

Revelation 2:10

Endurance

Do not envy sinners in your heart.
　　Instead, continue to fear the LORD.
　　　There is indeed a future,
　　　　and your hope will never be cut off.

Proverbs 23:17–18

So don't lose your confidence. It will bring you a great reward. You need endurance so that after you have done what God wants you to do, you can receive what he has promised.

Hebrews 10:35–36

My brothers and sisters, be very happy when you are tested in different ways. You know that such testing of your faith produces endurance.

James 1:2–3

Faith

Then Jesus called the crowd to himself along with his disciples. He said to them, "Those who want to follow me must say no to the things they want, pick up their crosses, and follow me. Those who want to save their lives will lose them. But those who lose their lives for me and for the Good News will save them."

Mark 8:34–35

Those who believe in him won't be condemned. But those who don't believe are already condemned because they don't believe in God's only Son.

John 3:18

I'm not ashamed of the Good News. It is God's power to save everyone who believes, Jews first and Greeks as well. God's approval is revealed in this Good News. This approval begins and ends with faith as Scripture says, "The person who has God's approval will live by faith."

Romans 1:16–17

Now, the way to receive God's approval has been made plain in a way other than Moses' Teachings. Moses' Teachings and the Prophets tell us this. Everyone who believes has God's approval through faith in Jesus Christ. There is no difference between people. Because all people have sinned, they have fallen short of God's glory. They receive God's approval freely by an act of his kindness through the price Christ Jesus paid to set us free from sin. God showed that Christ is the throne of mercy where God's approval is given through faith in Christ's blood. In his patience God waited to deal with sins committed in the past. He waited so that he could display his approval at the present time. This shows that he is a God of justice, a God who approves of people who believe in Jesus.

Romans 3:21–26

Is God only the God of the Jews? Isn't he also the God of people who are not Jewish? Certainly, he is, since it is the same God who approves circumcised people by faith and uncircumcised people through this same faith.

Romans 3:29–30

When people work, their pay is not regarded as a gift but something they have earned. However, when people don't work but believe God, the one who approves ungodly people, their faith is regarded as God's approval.

Romans 4:4–5

So it was not by obeying Moses' Teachings that Abraham or his descendants received the promise that he would inherit the world. Rather, it was through God's approval of his faith.

Romans 4:13

But the words "his faith was regarded as God's approval of him" were written not only for him but also for us. Our faith will be regarded as God's approval of us who believe in the one who brought Jesus, our Lord, back to life. Jesus, our Lord, was handed over to death because of our failures and was brought back to life so that we could receive God's approval.

Romans 4:23–25

Abraham serves as an example. He believed God, and that faith was regarded by God to be his approval of Abraham. You must understand that people who have faith are Abraham's descendants. Scripture saw ahead of time that God would give his approval to non-Jewish people who have faith. So Scripture announced the Good News to Abraham ahead of time when it said, "Through you all the people of the world will be blessed." So people who believe are blessed together with Abraham, the man of faith.

Galatians 3:6–9

No one receives God's approval by obeying the law's standards since, "The person who has God's approval will live by faith."

Galatians 3:11

These things that I once considered valuable, I now consider worthless for Christ. It's far more than that! I consider everything else worthless because I'm much better off knowing Christ Jesus my Lord. It's because of him that I think of everything as worthless. I threw it all away in order to gain Christ and to have a relationship with him. This means that I didn't receive God's approval by obeying his laws. The opposite is true! I have God's approval through faith in Christ. This is the approval that comes from God and is based on faith that knows Christ. Faith knows the power that his coming back to life gives and what it means to share his suffering. In this way I'm becoming like him in his death, with the confidence that I'll come back to life from the dead.

Philippians 3:7–11

Jesus Christ is the same yesterday, today, and forever.

Hebrews 13:8

Desire God's pure word as newborn babies desire milk. Then you will grow in your salvation. Certainly you have tasted that the Lord is good!

1 Peter 2:2–3

Those who love other believers live in the light. Nothing will destroy the faith of those who live in the light.

1 John 2:10

The person who acknowledges the Son also has the Father.

1 John 2:23

We have seen and testify to the fact that the Father sent his Son as the Savior of the world. God lives in those who declare that Jesus is the Son of God, and they live in God.

1 John 4:14–15

To love God means that we obey his commandments. Obeying his commandments isn't difficult because everyone who has been born from God has won the victory over the world. Our faith is what wins the victory over the world. Who wins the victory over the world? Isn't it the person who believes that Jesus is the Son of God?

1 John 5:3–5

Obedience

I will give you a new heart and put a new spirit in you. I will remove your stubborn hearts and give you obedient hearts. I will put my Spirit in you. I will enable you to live by my laws, and you will obey my rules. Then you will live in the land that I gave your ancestors. You will be my people, and I will be your God.

Ezekiel 36:26–28

Whoever knows and obeys my commandments is the person who loves me. Those who love me will have my Father's love, and I, too, will love them and show myself to them.

John 14:21

Jesus answered him, "Those who love me will do what I say. My Father will love them, and we will go to them and make our home with them."

John 14:23

I have loved you the same way the Father has loved me. So live in my love. If you obey my commandments, you will live in my love. I have obeyed my Father's commandments, and in that way I live in his love. I have told you this so that you will be as joyful as I am, and your joy will be complete. Love each other as I have loved you. This is what I'm commanding you to do. The greatest love you can show is to give your life for your friends.

John 15:9–13

In the same way, brothers and sisters, you have died to the laws in Moses' Teachings through Christ's body. You belong to someone else, the one who was brought back to life. As a result, we can do what God wants.

Romans 7:4–5

No one receives God's approval by obeying the law's standards since, "The person who has God's approval will live by faith."

Galatians 3:11

Children, obey your parents because you are Christians. This is the right thing to do. "Honor your father and mother that everything may go well for you, and you may have a long life on earth." This is an important commandment with a promise.

Ephesians 6:1–3

My dear friends, you have always obeyed, not only when I was with you but even more now that I'm absent. In the same way continue to work out your salvation with fear and trembling. It is God who produces in you the desires and actions that please him.

Philippians 2:12–13

Slaves, always obey your earthly masters. Don't obey them only while you're being watched, as if you merely wanted to please people. Be sincere in your motives out of respect for your real master. Whatever you do, do it wholeheartedly as though you were working for your real master and not merely for humans. You know that your real master will give you an inheritance as your reward. It is Christ, your real master, whom you are serving.

Colossians 3:22–24

Although Jesus was the Son of God, he learned to be obedient through his sufferings. After he had finished his work, he became the source of eternal salvation for everyone who obeys him.

Hebrews 5:8–9

However, the person who continues to study God's perfect teachings that make people free and who remains committed to them will be blessed. People like that don't merely listen and forget; they actually do what God's teachings say.

James 1:25

Love each other with a warm love that comes from the heart. After all, you have purified yourselves by obeying the truth. As a result you have a sincere love for each other. You have been born again, not from a seed that can be destroyed, but through God's everlasting word that can't be destroyed.

1 Peter 1:22–23

We are sure that we know Christ if we obey his commandments.

1 John 2:3

But whoever obeys what Christ says is the kind of person in whom God's love is perfected. That's how we know we are in Christ.

1 John 2:5

Those who obey Christ's commandments live in God, and God lives in them. We know that he lives in us because he has given us the Spirit.

1 John 3:24

To love God means that we obey his commandments. Obeying his commandments isn't difficult because everyone who has been born from God has won the victory over the world. Our faith is what wins the victory over the world. Who wins the victory over the world? Isn't it the person who believes that Jesus is the Son of God?

1 John 5:3–5

Patience

I waited patiently for the LORD.
  He turned to me and heard my cry for help.
  He pulled me out of a horrible pit,
    out of the mud and clay.
  He set my feet on a rock
    and made my steps secure.
  He placed a new song in my mouth,
    a song of praise to our God.
      Many will see this and worship.
      They will trust the LORD.

Psalm 40:1–3

The LORD is compassionate, merciful, patient,
  and always ready to forgive.

Psalm 103:8

The LORD is merciful, compassionate, patient,
  and always ready to forgive.

Psalm 145:8

Tear your hearts, not your clothes.
Return to the LORD your God.
He is merciful and compassionate,
patient, and always ready to forgive
and to change his plans about disaster.

Joel 2:13

God showed that Christ is the throne of mercy where
God's approval is given through faith in Christ's blood.
In his patience God waited to deal with sins committed
in the past. He waited so that he could display his approval at the present time. This shows that he is a God
of justice, a God who approves of people who believe
in Jesus.

Romans 3:25–26

I, a prisoner in the Lord, encourage you to live the kind
of life which proves that God has called you. Be humble
and gentle in every way. Be patient with each other and
lovingly accept each other. Through the peace that ties
you together, do your best to maintain the unity that
the Spirit gives. There is one body and one Spirit. In the
same way you were called to share one hope. There is
one Lord, one faith, one baptism, one God and Father
of all, who is over everything, through everything, and
in everything.

Ephesians 4:1–6

We want each of you to prove that you're working hard so that you will remain confident until the end. Then, instead of being lazy, you will imitate those who are receiving the promises through faith and patience.

Hebrews 6:11–12

You, too, must be patient. Don't give up hope. The Lord will soon be here.

James 5:8

The Lord isn't slow to do what he promised, as some people think. Rather, he is patient for your sake. He doesn't want to destroy anyone but wants all people to have an opportunity to turn to him and change the way they think and act.

2 Peter 3:9

Perseverance

Do not envy sinners in your heart.
  Instead, continue to fear the LORD.
    There is indeed a future,
      and your hope will never be cut off.

Proverbs 23:17–18

But that's not all. We also brag when we are suffering. We know that suffering creates endurance, endurance creates character, and character creates confidence. We're not ashamed to have this confidence, because God's love has been poured into our hearts by the Holy Spirit, who has been given to us.

Romans 5:3–5

Everything written long ago was written to teach us so that we would have confidence through the endurance and encouragement which the Scriptures give us.

Romans 15:4

There isn't any temptation that you have experienced which is unusual for humans. God, who faithfully keeps his promises, will not allow you to be tempted beyond your power to resist. But when you are tempted, he will also give you the ability to endure the temptation as your way of escape.

1 Corinthians 10:13

This is a statement that can be trusted:

If we have died with him, we will live with him.
If we endure, we will rule with him.
If we disown him, he will disown us.
If we are unfaithful, he remains faithful
    because he cannot be untrue to himself.

2 Timothy 2:11–13

We have been sprinkled with his blood to free us from a guilty conscience, and our bodies have been washed with clean water. So we must continue to come to him with a sincere heart and strong faith. We must continue to hold firmly to our declaration of faith. The one who made the promise is faithful.

Hebrews 10:22–23

So don't lose your confidence. It will bring you a great reward. You need endurance so that after you have done what God wants you to do, you can receive what he has promised.

Hebrews 10:35–36

My brothers and sisters, be very happy when you are tested in different ways. You know that such testing of your faith produces endurance.

James 1:2–3

Those who suffer because that is God's will for them must entrust themselves to a faithful creator and continue to do what is good.

1 Peter 4:19

Don't be afraid of what you are going to suffer. The devil is going to throw some of you into prison so that you may be tested. Your suffering will go on for ten days. Be faithful until death, and I will give you the crown of life.

Revelation 2:10

Perspective of God's Kingdom

Jesus said, "I can guarantee this truth: Anyone who gave up his home, brothers, sisters, mother, father, children, or fields because of me and the Good News will certainly receive a hundred times as much here in this life. They will certainly receive homes, brothers, sisters, mothers, children and fields, along with persecutions. But in the world to come they will receive eternal life. But many who are first will be last, and the last will be first."

Mark 10:29–31

Don't be afraid, little flock. Your Father is pleased to give you the kingdom.

Luke 12:32

He died for all people so that those who live should no longer live for themselves but for the man who died and was brought back to life for them.

2 Corinthians 5:15

Remember this: The farmer who plants a few seeds will have a very small harvest. But the farmer who plants because he has received God's blessings will receive a harvest of God's blessings in return. Each of you should give whatever you have decided. You shouldn't be sorry that you gave or feel forced to give, since God loves a cheerful giver. Besides, God will give you his constantly overflowing kindness. Then, when you always have everything you need, you can do more and more good things. Scripture says,

> "The righteous person gives freely to the poor.
> His righteousness continues forever."

God gives seed to the farmer and food to those who need to eat. God will also give you seed and multiply it. In your lives he will increase the things you do that have his approval. God will make you rich enough so that you can always be generous. Your generosity will produce thanksgiving to God because of us. What you do to serve others not only provides for the needs of God's people, but also produces more and more prayers of thanksgiving to God. You will honor God through this genuine act of service because of your commitment to spread the Good News of Christ and because of your generosity in sharing with them and everyone else. With deep affection they will pray for you because of the extreme kindness that God has shown you. I thank God for his gift that words cannot describe.

2 Corinthians 9:6–15

That is why you are no longer foreigners and outsiders but citizens together with God's people and members of God's family. You are built on the foundation of the apostles and prophets. Christ Jesus himself is the cornerstone. In him all the parts of the building fit together and grow into a holy temple in the Lord. Through him you, also, are being built in the Spirit together with others into a place where God lives.

Ephesians 2:19–22

Once you lived in the dark, but now the Lord has filled you with light. Live as children who have light.

Ephesians 5:8

Live as citizens who reflect the Good News about Christ. Then, whether I come to see you or whether I stay away, I'll hear all about you. I'll hear that you are firmly united in spirit, united in fighting for the faith that the Good News brings.

Philippians 1:27

We have been set apart as holy because Jesus Christ did what God wanted him to do by sacrificing his body once and for all.

Hebrews 10:10

However, you are chosen people, a royal priesthood, a holy nation, people who belong to God. You were chosen to tell about the excellent qualities of God, who called you out of darkness into his marvelous light. Once you were not God's people, but now you are. Once you were not shown mercy, but now you have been shown mercy.

1 Peter 2:9–10

I'm writing to you, dear children, because your sins are forgiven through Christ. I'm writing to you, fathers, because you know Christ who has existed from the beginning. I'm writing to you, young people, because you have won the victory over the evil one. I've written to you, children, because you know the Father. I've written to you, fathers, because you know Christ, who has existed from the beginning. I've written to you, young people, because you are strong and God's word lives in you. You have won the victory over the evil one.

1 John 2:12–14

We understand what love is when we realize that Christ gave his life for us. That means we must give our lives for other believers.

1 John 3:16

I will make everyone who wins the victory a pillar in the temple of my God. They will never leave it again. I will write on them the name of my God, the name of the city of my God (the New Jerusalem coming down out of heaven from my God), and my new name.

Revelation 3:12

You bought people with your blood to be God's
   own.
   They are from every tribe, language, people,
      and nation.
You made them a kingdom and priests for our
   God.
   They will rule as kings on the earth.

Revelation 5:9–10

The angel showed me a river filled with the water of
life, as clear as crystal. It was flowing from the throne
of God and the lamb. Between the street of the city
and the river there was a tree of life visible from both
sides. It produced 12 kinds of fruit. Each month had its
own fruit. The leaves of the tree will heal the nations.
There will no longer be any curse. The throne of God
and the lamb will be in the city. His servants will worship him and see his face. His name will be on their
foreheads. There will be no more night, and they will
not need any light from lamps or the sun because the
Lord God will shine on them. They will rule as kings
forever and ever.

Revelation 22:1–5

Repentance

I baptize you with water so that you will change the way you think and act. But the one who comes after me is more powerful than I. I am not worthy to remove his sandals. He will baptize you with the Holy Spirit and fire.

Matthew 3:11

The Pharisees and their scribes complained to Jesus' disciples. They asked, "Why do you eat and drink with tax collectors and sinners?" Jesus answered them, "Healthy people don't need a doctor; those who are sick do. I've come to call sinners to change the way they think and act, not to call people who think they have God's approval."

Luke 5:30–31

Peter answered them, "All of you must turn to God and change the way you think and act, and each of you must be baptized in the name of Jesus Christ so that your sins will be forgiven. Then you will receive the Holy Spirit as a gift. This promise belongs to you and to your children and to everyone who is far away. It belongs to everyone who worships the Lord our God."

Acts 2:38–39

Don't become like the people of this world. Instead, change the way you think. Then you will always be able to determine what God really wants—what is good, pleasing, and perfect.

Romans 12:2

The Lord isn't slow to do what he promised, as some people think. Rather, he is patient for your sake. He doesn't want to destroy anyone but wants all people to have an opportunity to turn to him and change the way they think and act.

2 Peter 3:9

I correct and discipline everyone I love. Take this seriously and change the way you think and act.

Revelation 3:19

Salvation

So consider yourselves dead to sin's power but living for God in the power Christ Jesus gives you.

Romans 6:11

Now you have been freed from sin and have become God's slaves. This results in a holy life and, finally, in everlasting life. The payment for sin is death, but the gift that God freely gives is everlasting life found in Christ Jesus our Lord.

Romans 6:22–23

So those who are believers in Christ Jesus can no longer be condemned. The standards of the Spirit, who gives life through Christ Jesus, have set you free from the standards of sin and death.

Romans 8:1–2

Christ gives us confidence about you in God's presence. By ourselves we are not qualified in any way to claim that we can do anything. Rather, God makes us qualified. He has also qualified us to be ministers of a new promise, a spiritual promise, not a written one. Clearly, what was written brings death, but the Spirit brings life.

2 Corinthians 3:4–6

Whoever is a believer in Christ is a new creation. The old way of living has disappeared. A new way of living has come into existence. God has done all this. He has restored our relationship with him through Christ, and has given us this ministry of restoring relationships.

2 Corinthians 5:17–18

Training the body helps a little, but godly living helps in every way. Godly living has the promise of life now and in the world to come.

1 Timothy 4:8

After all, God's saving kindness has appeared for the benefit of all people. It trains us to avoid ungodly lives filled with worldly desires so that we can live self-controlled, moral, and godly lives in this present world.

Titus 2:11–12

God's divine power has given us everything we need for life and for godliness. This power was given to us through knowledge of the one who called us by his own glory and integrity. Through his glory and integrity he has given us his promises that are of the highest value. Through these promises you will share in the divine nature because you have escaped the corruption that sinful desires cause in the world.

2 Peter 1:3–4

Trust

You have seen it; yes, you have taken note of
    trouble and grief
    and placed them under your control.
        The victim entrusts himself to you.
You alone have been the helper of orphans.

                    Psalm 10:14

We wait for the LORD.
    He is our help and our shield.
    In him our hearts find joy.
    In his holy name we trust.

            Psalm 33:20–21

It is better to depend on the LORD
    than to trust mortals.

            Psalm 118:8

Trust the LORD with all your heart,
  and do not rely on your own understanding.
In all your ways acknowledge him,
  and he will make your paths smooth.

Proverbs 3:5–6

Whoever gives attention to the LORD's word
    prospers,
  and blessed is the person who trusts the LORD.

Proverbs 16:20

Trust the LORD always,
  because the LORD, the LORD alone, is an
    everlasting rock.

Isaiah 26:4

God's Promises Guide Me in . . .

Change

The LORD's plan stands firm forever.
His thoughts stand firm in every generation.

Psalm 33:11

Say to the nations, "The LORD rules as king!"
The earth stands firm; it cannot be moved.
He will judge people fairly.

Psalm 96:10

You set the earth on its foundations
   so that it can never be shaken.

Psalm 104:5

He provides food for those who fear him.
He always remembers his promise.

Psalm 111:5

"The mountains may move, and the hills may
   shake,
   but my kindness will never depart from you.
   My promise of peace will never change,"
      says the LORD, who has compassion on you.

Isaiah 54:10

With perfect peace you will protect those whose
   minds cannot be changed,
   because they trust you.

Isaiah 56:3

I, the LORD, never change. That is why you descendants of Jacob haven't been destroyed yet.

Malachi 3:6

I baptize you with water so that you will change the
way you think and act. But the one who comes after
me is more powerful than I. I am not worthy to remove
his sandals. He will baptize you with the Holy Spirit
and fire.

Matthew 3:11

The Pharisees and their scribes complained to Jesus'
disciples. They asked, "Why do you eat and drink
with tax collectors and sinners?" Jesus answered them,
"Healthy people don't need a doctor; those who are
sick do. I've come to call sinners to change the way they
think and act, not to call people who think they have
God's approval."

Luke 5:30–31

Peter answered them, "All of you must turn to God and
change the way you think and act, and each of you must
be baptized in the name of Jesus Christ so that your sins
will be forgiven. Then you will receive the Holy Spirit as
a gift. This promise belongs to you and to your children

and to everyone who is far away. It belongs to everyone who worships the Lord our God."

I'm telling you a mystery. Not all of us will die, but we will all be changed. It will happen in an instant, in a split second at the sound of the last trumpet. Indeed, that trumpet will sound, and then the dead will come back to life. They will be changed so that they can live forever. This body that decays must be changed into a body that cannot decay. This mortal body must be changed into a body that will live forever. When this body that decays is changed into a body that cannot decay, and this mortal body is changed into a body that will live forever, then the teaching of Scripture will come true:

> "Death is turned into victory!
> Death, where is your victory?
> Death, where is your sting?"

Sin gives death its sting, and God's standards give sin its power. Thank God that he gives us the victory through our Lord Jesus Christ.

1 Corinthians 15:51–57

As all of us reflect the Lord's glory with faces that are not covered with veils, we are being changed into his image with ever-increasing glory. This comes from the Lord, who is the Spirit.

2 Corinthians 3:18

We, however, are citizens of heaven. We look forward to the Lord Jesus Christ coming from heaven as our Savior. Through his power to bring everything under his authority, he will change our humble bodies and make them like his glorified body.

Philippians 3:20–21

When people take oaths, they base their oaths on someone greater than themselves. Their oaths guarantee what they say and end all arguments. God wouldn't change his plan. He wanted to make this perfectly clear to those who would receive his promise, so he took an oath. God did this so that we would be encouraged. God cannot lie when he takes an oath or makes a promise. These two things can never be changed. Those of us who have taken refuge in him hold on to the confidence we have been given. We have this confidence as a sure and strong anchor for our lives. This confidence goes into the holy place behind the curtain where Jesus went before us on our behalf. He has become the chief priest forever in the way Melchizedek was a priest.

Hebrews 6:16–20

Every good present and every perfect gift comes from above, from the Father who made the sun, moon, and stars. The Father doesn't change like the shifting shadows produced by the sun and the moon.

James 1:17

I correct and discipline everyone I love. Take this seriously and change the way you think and act.

Revelation 3:19

Decisions

Trust the LORD with all your heart,
    and do not rely on your own understanding.
In all your ways acknowledge him,
    and he will make your paths smooth.

Proverbs 3:5–6

At the same time the Spirit also helps us in our weakness, because we don't know how to pray for what we need. But the Spirit intercedes along with our groans that cannot be expressed in words. The one who searches our hearts knows what the Spirit has in mind. The Spirit intercedes for God's people the way God wants him to.

Romans 8:26–27

Don't become like the people of this world. Instead, change the way you think. Then you will always be able to determine what God really wants—what is good, pleasing, and perfect.

Romans 12:2

Since you were brought back to life with Christ, focus on the things that are above—where Christ holds the highest position. Keep your mind on things above, not on worldly things. You have died, and your life is hidden with Christ in God. Christ is your life. When he appears, then you, too, will appear with him in glory.

Colossians 3:1–4

If any of you needs wisdom to know what you should do, you should ask God, and he will give it to you. God is generous to everyone and doesn't find fault with them.

James 1:5

Fear of the Lord

Your kindness is so great!
> You reserve it for those who fear you.
>> Adam's descendants watch
>>> as you show it to those who take refuge in
>>> you.
> You hide them in the secret place of your
> presence
> from those who scheme against them.
> You keep them in a shelter,
>> safe from quarrelsome tongues.

Psalm 31:19–20

The Messenger of the LORD camps around those
who fear him,
and he rescues them.

Psalm 34:7

Fear the LORD, you holy people who belong to him.
Those who fear him are never in need.
Young lions go hungry and may starve,
but those who seek the LORD's help have all the
good things they need.

Psalm 34:9–10

O God, you have heard my vows.
    You have given me the inheritance
        that belongs to those who fear your name.

Psalm 61:5

But from everlasting to everlasting,
    the LORD's mercy is on those who fear him.
    His righteousness belongs
        to their children and grandchildren,

Psalm 103:17

He provides food for those who fear him.
He always remembers his promise.

Psalm 111:5

If you fear the LORD, trust the LORD.
    He is your helper and your shield.

Psalm 115:11

He will bless those who fear the LORD,
    from the least important to the most
        important.

Psalm 115:13

O LORD, who would be able to stand
    if you kept a record of sins?
But with you there is forgiveness
    so that you can be feared.

Psalm 130:3–4

He fills the needs of those who fear him.
He hears their cries for help and saves them.

Psalm 145:19

On the heels of humility (the fear of the LORD)
are riches and honor and life.

Proverbs 22:4

Do not envy sinners in your heart.
Instead, continue to fear the LORD.
There is indeed a future,
and your hope will never be cut off.

Proverbs 23:17–18

My dear friends, you have always obeyed, not only when
I was with you but even more now that I'm absent. In
the same way continue to work out your salvation with
fear and trembling. It is God who produces in you the
desires and actions that please him.

Philippians 2:12–13

Lord, who won't fear and praise your name?
You are the only holy one,
and all the nations will come to worship you
because they know about your fair
judgments.

Revelation 15:3–4

Fruitfulness

I am the vine. You are the branches. Those who live in me while I live in them will produce a lot of fruit. But you can't produce anything without me.

John 15:5

If you live in me and what I say lives in you, then ask for anything you want, and it will be yours. You give glory to my Father when you produce a lot of fruit and therefore show that you are my disciples.

John 15:7–8

You didn't choose me, but I chose you. I have appointed you to go, to produce fruit that will last, and to ask the Father in my name to give you whatever you ask for.

John 15:16

Jesus Christ will fill your lives with everything that God's approval produces. Your lives will then bring glory and praise to God.

Philippians 1:11

Giving to God

I will proclaim the name of the LORD.
Give our God the greatness he deserves!
  He is a rock.
    What he does is perfect.
      All his ways are fair.
  He is a faithful God, who does no wrong.
    He is honorable and reliable.

Deuteronomy 32:3–4

Give your contributions privately. Your Father sees what you do in private. He will reward you.

Matthew 6:4

When you pray, go to your room and close the door. Pray privately to your Father who is with you. Your Father sees what you do in private. He will reward you.

Matthew 6:6

Then your fasting won't be obvious. Instead, it will be obvious to your Father who is with you in private. Your Father sees what you do in private. He will reward you.

Matthew 6:18

Remember this: The farmer who plants a few seeds will have a very small harvest. But the farmer who plants because he has received God's blessings will receive a harvest of God's blessings in return. Each of you should give whatever you have decided. You shouldn't be sorry that you gave or feel forced to give, since God loves a cheerful giver. Besides, God will give you his constantly overflowing kindness. Then, when you always have everything you need, you can do more and more good things. Scripture says,

> "The righteous person gives freely to the poor.
> His righteousness continues forever."

God gives seed to the farmer and food to those who need to eat. God will also give you seed and multiply it. In your lives he will increase the things you do that have his approval. God will make you rich enough so that you can always be generous. Your generosity will produce thanksgiving to God because of us. What you do to serve others not only provides for the needs of God's people, but also produces more and more prayers of thanksgiving to God. You will honor God through this genuine act of service because of your commitment to spread the Good News of Christ and because of your generosity in sharing with them and everyone else. With deep affection they will pray for you because of the extreme kindness that God has shown you. I thank God for his gift that words cannot describe.

2 Corinthians 9:6–15

Honesty

Never steal, lie, or deceive your neighbor.

Leviticus 19:11

Who may go up the LORD's mountain?
Who may stand in his holy place?
  The one who has clean hands and a pure heart
    and does not long for what is false
      or lie when he is under oath.
  This person will receive a blessing from the
    LORD
    and righteousness from God, his savior.

Psalm 24:3–5

Better a few possessions gained honestly
  than many gained through injustice.

Proverbs 16:8

Better to be a poor person who lives innocently
  than to be one who talks dishonestly and is
    a fool.

Proverbs 19:1

The person who does what is right and speaks the
truth will live.
He rejects getting rich by extortion and refuses
to take bribes.
He refuses to listen to those who are plotting
murders.
He doesn't look for evil things to do.
This person will live on high.
His stronghold will be a fortress made of rock.
He will have plenty of food
and a dependable supply of water.

Isaiah 33:15–16

Finally, brothers and sisters, keep your thoughts on whatever is right or deserves praise: things that are true, honorable, fair, pure, acceptable, or commendable. Practice what you've learned and received from me, what you heard and saw me do. Then the God who gives this peace will be with you.

Philippians 4:8–9

Don't lie to each other. You've gotten rid of the person you used to be and the life you used to live, and you've become a new person. This new person is continually renewed in knowledge to be like its Creator.

Colossians 3:9–10

Humility

If my people, who are called by my name,
   will humble themselves,
      pray, search for me, and turn from their evil
         ways,
then I will hear their prayer from heaven, forgive
      their sins,
   and heal their country.

2 Chronicles 7:14

The LORD is near to those whose hearts are
      humble.
He saves those whose spirits are crushed.

Psalm 34:18

He brings about justice for those who are
      oppressed.
He gives food to those who are hungry.
The LORD sets prisoners free.

Psalm 146:7

He is the healer of the brokenhearted.
He is the one who bandages their wounds.

Psalm 147:3

Arrogance comes,
   then comes shame,
      but wisdom remains with humble people.

Proverbs 11:2

On the heels of humility (the fear of the Lord)
   are riches and honor and life.

Proverbs 22:4

He will gladly bear the fear of the Lord.
He will not judge by what his eyes see
   or decide by what his ears hear.
He will judge the poor justly.
He will make fair decisions for the humble people
   on earth.
He will strike the earth with a rod from his
   mouth.
He will kill the wicked with the breath from his
   lips.
   Justice will be the belt around his waist.
   Faithfulness will be the belt around his hips.

Isaiah 11:3–5

Sing with joy, you heavens!
Rejoice, you earth!
Break into shouts of joy, you mountains!

The LORD has comforted his people
    and will have compassion on his humble
        people.

Isaiah 49:13

The High and Lofty One lives forever, and his
    name is holy.
This is what he says:
    I live in a high and holy place.
        But I am with those who are crushed and
            humble.
            I will renew the spirit of those who are
                humble
                and the courage of those who are
                    crushed.
    I will not accuse you forever.
    I will not be angry with you forever.
        Otherwise, the spirits, the lives of those I've
            made,
            would grow faint in my presence.

Isaiah 57:15–16

If you give some of your own food to feed those
    who are hungry
    and to satisfy the needs of those who are
        humble,
then your light will rise in the dark,
    and your darkness will become as bright as the
        noonday sun.

Isaiah 58:10

The Spirit of the Almighty LORD is with me
because the LORD has anointed me
to deliver good news to humble people.
He has sent me
to heal those who are brokenhearted,
to announce that captives will be set free
and prisoners will be released.
He has sent me
to announce the year of the LORD's good will
and the day of our God's vengeance,
to comfort all those who grieve.
He has sent me
to provide for all those who grieve in Zion,
to give them crowns instead of ashes,
the oil of joy instead of tears of grief,
and clothes of praise instead of a spirit
of weakness.

Isaiah 61:1–3

I will pay attention to those
who are humble and sorry for their sins
and who tremble at my word.

Isaiah 66:2

I can guarantee this truth: Whoever gives any of my humble followers a cup of cold water because that person is my disciple will certainly never lose his reward.

Matthew 10:42

Come to me, all who are tired from carrying heavy loads, and I will give you rest. Place my yoke over your shoulders, and learn from me, because I am gentle and humble. Then you will find rest for yourselves because my yoke is easy and my burden is light.

Matthew 11:28–30

I, a prisoner in the Lord, encourage you to live the kind of life which proves that God has called you. Be humble and gentle in every way. Be patient with each other and lovingly accept each other. Through the peace that ties you together, do your best to maintain the unity that the Spirit gives. There is one body and one Spirit. In the same way you were called to share one hope. There is one Lord, one faith, one baptism, one God and Father of all, who is over everything, through everything, and in everything.

Ephesians 4:1–6

Humble yourselves in the Lord's presence. Then he will give you a high position.

James 4:10

Be humbled by God's power so that when the right time comes he will honor you.

1 Peter 5:6

Money

Fear the LORD, you holy people who belong to
him.
Those who fear him are never in need.
Young lions go hungry and may starve,
but those who seek the LORD's help have all the
good things they need.

Psalm 34:9–10

The LORD will certainly give us what is good,
and our land will produce crops.
Righteousness will go ahead of him
and make a path for his steps.

Psalm 85:12–13

The eyes of all creatures look to you,
and you give them their food at the proper
time.
You open your hand,
and you satisfy the desire of every living
thing.

Psalm 145:15–16

He fills the needs of those who fear him.
He hears their cries for help and saves them.

Psalm 145:19

Don't ever worry and say, "What are we going to eat?" or "What are we going to drink?" or "What are we going to wear?" Everyone is concerned about these things, and your heavenly Father certainly knows you need all of them. But first, be concerned about his kingdom and what has his approval. Then all these things will be provided for you.

Matthew 6:31–33

Then Jesus said to his disciples, "So I tell you to stop worrying about what you will eat or wear. Life is more than food, and the body is more than clothes. Consider the crows. They don't plant or harvest. They don't even have a storeroom or a barn. Yet, God feeds them. You are worth much more than birds."

Luke 12:22–24

That's the way God clothes the grass in the field. Today it's alive, and tomorrow it's thrown into an incinerator. So how much more will he clothe you people who have so little faith?

Luke 12:28

My God will richly fill your every need in a glorious way through Christ Jesus. Glory belongs to our God and Father forever! Amen.

Philippians 4:19–20

A godly life brings huge profits to people who are content with what they have. We didn't bring anything into the world, and we can't take anything out of it. As long as we have food and clothes, we should be satisfied.

1 Timothy 6:6–8

Don't love money. Be happy with what you have because God has said, "I will never abandon you or leave you." So we can confidently say,

> "The Lord is my helper.
> I will not be afraid.
> What can mortals do to me?"

Hebrews 13:5–6

Prayer

When I am in trouble, I call out to you
  because you answer me.

Psalm 86:7

When you call to me, I will answer you.
  I will be with you when you are in trouble.
  I will save you and honor you.
  I will satisfy you with a long life.
  I will show you how I will save you.

Psalm 91:15–16

When the LORD builds Zion,
  he will appear in his glory.
  He will turn his attention to the prayers
    of those who have been abandoned.
  He will not despise their prayers.

Psalm 102:16–17

The LORD is near to everyone who prays to him,
  to every faithful person who prays to him.

Psalm 145:18

Call to me, and I will answer you. I will tell you great and mysterious things that you do not know.

Jeremiah 33:3

I will look to the Lord.
I will wait for God to save me.
I will wait for my God to listen to me.

Micah 7:7

Ask, and you will receive. Search, and you will find. Knock, and the door will be opened for you. Everyone who asks will receive. The one who searches will find, and for the one who knocks, the door will be opened.

Matthew 7:7–8

Have faith that you will receive whatever you ask for in prayer.

Matthew 21:22

Jesus said to him, "As far as possibilities go, everything is possible for the person who believes."

Mark 9:23

Jesus said to them, "Have faith in God! I can guarantee this truth: This is what will be done for someone who doesn't doubt but believes what he says will happen: He can say to this mountain, 'Be uprooted and thrown into the sea,' and it will be done for him. That's why I tell you to have faith that you have already received whatever you pray for, and it will be yours."

Mark 11:22–24

I will do anything you ask the Father in my name so that the Father will be given glory because of the Son. If you ask me to do something, I will do it.

John 14:13–14

If you live in me and what I say lives in you, then ask for anything you want, and it will be yours. You give glory to my Father when you produce a lot of fruit and therefore show that you are my disciples.

John 15:7–8

You didn't choose me, but I chose you. I have appointed you to go, to produce fruit that will last, and to ask the Father in my name to give you whatever you ask for.

John 15:16

Now that we have God's approval by faith, we have peace with God because of what our Lord Jesus Christ has done. Through Christ we can approach God and stand in his favor. So we brag because of our confidence that we will receive glory from God.

Romans 5:1–2

At the same time the Spirit also helps us in our weakness, because we don't know how to pray for what we need. But the Spirit intercedes along with our groans that cannot be expressed in words. The one who searches our hearts knows what the Spirit has in mind. The Spirit intercedes for God's people the way God wants him to.

Romans 8:26–27

Always be joyful in the Lord! I'll say it again: Be joyful! Let everyone know how considerate you are. The Lord is near. Never worry about anything. But in every situation let God know what you need in prayers and requests while giving thanks. Then God's peace, which goes beyond anything we can imagine, will guard your thoughts and emotions through Christ Jesus.

Philippians 4:4–7

If any of you are having trouble, pray. If you are happy, sing psalms. If you are sick, call for the church leaders. Have them pray for you and anoint you with olive oil in the name of the Lord. (Prayers offered in faith will save those who are sick, and the Lord will cure them.) If you have sinned, you will be forgiven. So admit your sins to each other, and pray for each other so that you will be healed.

James 5:13–16

The Lord's eyes are on those who do what he
    approves.
    His ears hear their prayer.
    The Lord confronts those who do evil.

1 Peter 3:12

My dear children, I'm writing this to you so that you will not sin. Yet, if anyone does sin, we have Jesus Christ, who has God's full approval. He speaks on our behalf when we come into the presence of the Father. He is the payment for our sins, and not only for our sins, but also for the sins of the whole world.

1 John 2:1–2

We are confident that God listens to us if we ask for anything that has his approval. We know that he listens to our requests. So we know that we already have what we ask him for.

1 John 5:14–15

Purpose

I know the plans that I have for you, declares the Lord.
They are plans for peace and not disaster, plans to give
you a future filled with hope. Then you will call to me.
You will come and pray to me, and I will hear you. When
you look for me, you will find me.

Jeremiah 29:11–13

I will give you a new heart and put a new spirit in you. I
will remove your stubborn hearts and give you obedient
hearts. I will put my Spirit in you. I will enable you to
live by my laws, and you will obey my rules. Then you
will live in the land that I gave your ancestors. You will
be my people, and I will be your God.

Ezekiel 36:26–28

Then I will give all people pure lips
   to worship the Lord
      and to serve him with one purpose.

Zephaniah 3:9

We know that all things work together for the good of those who love God—those whom he has called according to his plan.

Romans 8:28

Our bodies have many parts, but these parts don't all do the same thing. In the same way, even though we are many individuals, Christ makes us one body and individuals who are connected to each other.

Romans 12:4–5

Through the blood of his Son, we are set free from our sins. God forgives our failures because of his overflowing kindness. He poured out his kindness by giving us every kind of wisdom and insight when he revealed the mystery of his plan to us. He had decided to do this through Christ.

Ephesians 1:7–9

He also gave apostles, prophets, missionaries, as well as pastors and teachers as gifts to his church. Their purpose is to prepare God's people to serve and to build up the body of Christ. This is to continue until all of us are united in our faith and in our knowledge about God's Son, until we become mature, until we measure up to Christ, who is the standard.

Ephesians 4:11–13

He makes the whole body fit together and unites it through the support of every joint. As each and every part does its job, he makes the body grow so that it builds itself up in love.

Ephesians 4:16

Christ makes the whole body grow as God wants it to, through support and unity given by the joints and ligaments.

Colossians 2:19

Christ carried our sins in his body on the cross so that freed from our sins, we could live a life that has God's approval. His wounds have healed you. You were like lost sheep. Now you have come back to the shepherd and bishop of your lives.

1 Peter 2:24–25

You bought people with your blood to be God's
own.
They are from every tribe, language, people,
and nation.
You made them a kingdom and priests for our
God.
They will rule as kings on the earth.

Revelation 5:9–10

Relationships

Blessed is the one who has concern for helpless
people.
The LORD will rescue him in times of trouble.
The LORD will protect him and keep him alive.
He will be blessed in the land.
Do not place him at the mercy of his
enemies.
The LORD will support him on his sickbed.
You will restore this person to health when
he is ill.

Psalm 41:1–3

I have loved you the same way the Father has loved me.
So live in my love. If you obey my commandments, you
will live in my love. I have obeyed my Father's commandments, and in that way I live in his love. I have told you
this so that you will be as joyful as I am, and your joy
will be complete. Love each other as I have loved you.
This is what I'm commanding you to do. The greatest
love you can show is to give your life for your friends.

John 15:9–13

I, a prisoner in the Lord, encourage you to live the kind of life which proves that God has called you. Be humble and gentle in every way. Be patient with each other and lovingly accept each other. Through the peace that ties you together, do your best to maintain the unity that the Spirit gives. There is one body and one Spirit. In the same way you were called to share one hope. There is one Lord, one faith, one baptism, one God and Father of all, who is over everything, through everything, and in everything.

Ephesians 4:1–6

He makes the whole body fit together and unites it through the support of every joint. As each and every part does its job, he makes the body grow so that it builds itself up in love.

Ephesians 4:16

Husbands, love your wives as Christ loved the church and gave his life for it. He did this to make the church holy by cleansing it, washing it using water along with spoken words. Then he could present it to himself as a glorious church, without any kind of stain or wrinkle— holy and without faults.

Ephesians 5:25–27

Children, obey your parents because you are Christians. This is the right thing to do. "Honor your father and mother that everything may go well for you, and you may have a long life on earth." This is an important commandment with a promise.

Ephesians 6:1–3

Always be joyful in the Lord! I'll say it again: Be joyful! Let everyone know how considerate you are. The Lord is near. Never worry about anything. But in every situation let God know what you need in prayers and requests while giving thanks. Then God's peace, which goes beyond anything we can imagine, will guard your thoughts and emotions through Christ Jesus.

Philippians 4:4–7

I want you to know how hard I work for you, for the people of Laodicea, and for people I have never met. Because they are united in love, I work so that they may be encouraged by all the riches that come from a complete understanding of Christ. He is the mystery of God.

Colossians 2:1–2

Christ makes the whole body grow as God wants it to, through support and unity given by the joints and ligaments.

Colossians 2:19

Slaves, always obey your earthly masters. Don't obey them only while you're being watched, as if you merely wanted to please people. Be sincere in your motives out of respect for your real master. Whatever you do, do it wholeheartedly as though you were working for your real master and not merely for humans. You know that your real master will give you an inheritance as your reward. It is Christ, your real master, whom you are serving.

Colossians 3:22–24

We also pray that the Lord will greatly increase your love for each other and for everyone else, just as we love you. Then he will strengthen you to be holy. Then you will be blameless in the presence of our God and Father when our Lord Jesus comes with all God's holy people.

1 Thessalonians 3:12–13

You don't need anyone to write to you about the way Christians should love each other. God has taught you to love each other.

1 Thessalonians 4:9

Love each other with a warm love that comes from the heart. After all, you have purified yourselves by obeying the truth. As a result you have a sincere love for each other.

1 Peter 1:22

Above all, love each other warmly, because love covers many sins.

1 Peter 4:8

But if we live in the light in the same way that God is in the light, we have a relationship with each other. And the blood of his Son Jesus cleanses us from every sin.

1 John 1:7

Those who love other believers live in the light. Nothing will destroy the faith of those who live in the light.

1 John 2:10

We understand what love is when we realize that Christ gave his life for us. That means we must give our lives for other believers.

1 John 3:16

Dear friends, we must love each other because love comes from God. Everyone who loves has been born from God and knows God.

1 John 4:7

Responsibility

I can guarantee this truth: Whoever gives any of my humble followers a cup of cold water because that person is my disciple will certainly never lose his reward.

Matthew 10:42

Give, and you will receive. A large quantity, pressed together, shaken down, and running over will be put into your pocket. The standards you use for others will be applied to you.

Luke 6:38

Those who serve me must follow me. My servants will be with me wherever I will be. If people serve me, the Father will honor them.

John 12:26

Whoever knows and obeys my commandments is the person who loves me. Those who love me will have my Father's love, and I, too, will love them and show myself to them.

John 14:21

I have loved you the same way the Father has loved me. So live in my love. If you obey my commandments, you will live in my love. I have obeyed my Father's commandments, and in that way I live in his love. I have told you this so that you will be as joyful as I am, and your joy will be complete. Love each other as I have loved you. This is what I'm commanding you to do. The greatest love you can show is to give your life for your friends.

John 15:9–13

You didn't choose me, but I chose you. I have appointed you to go, to produce fruit that will last, and to ask the Father in my name to give you whatever you ask for.

John 15:16

He will continue to give you strength until the end so that no one can accuse you of anything on the day of our Lord Jesus Christ. God faithfully keeps his promises. He called you to be partners with his Son Jesus Christ our Lord.

1 Corinthians 1:8–9

Jesus Christ will fill your lives with everything that God's approval produces. Your lives will then bring glory and praise to God.

Philippians 1:11

Live as citizens who reflect the Good News about Christ. Then, whether I come to see you or whether I stay away, I'll hear all about you. I'll hear that you are firmly united in spirit, united in fighting for the faith that the Good News brings.

Philippians 1:27

You know very well that we treated each of you the way a father treats his children. We comforted you and encouraged you. Yet, we insisted that you should live in a way that proves you belong to the God who calls you into his kingdom and glory.

1 Thessalonians 2:11–12

In the past God spoke to our ancestors at many different times and in many different ways through the prophets. In these last days he has spoken to us through his Son. God made his Son responsible for everything. His Son is the one through whom God made the universe.

Hebrews 1:1–2

However, you are chosen people, a royal priesthood, a holy nation, people who belong to God. You were chosen to tell about the excellent qualities of God, who called you out of darkness into his marvelous light. Once you were not God's people, but now you are. Once you were not shown mercy, but now you have been shown mercy.

1 Peter 2:9–10

Keep your mind clear, and be alert. Your opponent the devil is prowling around like a roaring lion as he looks for someone to devour. Be firm in the faith and resist him, knowing that other believers throughout the world are going through the same kind of suffering. God, who shows you his kindness and who has called you through Christ Jesus to his eternal glory, will restore you, strengthen you, make you strong, and support you as you suffer for a little while.

1 Peter 5:8–10

Wisdom

Do not boast
> or let arrogance come out of your mouth
>> because the LORD is a God of knowledge,
>> and he weighs our actions.

1 Samuel 2:3

Your righteousness is like the mountains of God,
> your judgments like the deep ocean.
>> You save people and animals, O LORD.

Psalm 36:6

The mouth of the righteous person reflects on
> wisdom.
> His tongue speaks what is fair.
The teachings of his God are in his heart.
> His feet do not slip.

Psalm 37:30–31

Our Lord is great, and his power is great.
There is no limit to his understanding.

Psalm 147:5

The LORD gives wisdom.
> From his mouth come knowledge and
> > understanding.
> > He has reserved priceless wisdom for decent
> > people.
He is a shield for those who walk in integrity
> in order to guard those on paths of justice
> > and to watch over the way of his godly ones.

Proverbs 2:6–8

Arrogance comes,
> then comes shame,
> > but wisdom remains with humble people.

Proverbs 11:2

Then a shoot will come out from the stump of
> Jesse,
> and a branch from its roots will bear fruit.
The Spirit of the LORD will rest on him—
> the Spirit of wisdom and understanding,
> the Spirit of advice and power,
> the Spirit of knowledge and fear of the LORD.

Isaiah 11:1–2

Through the blood of his Son, we are set free from our sins. God forgives our failures because of his overflowing kindness. He poured out his kindness by giving us every kind of wisdom and insight when he revealed the mystery of his plan to us. He had decided to do this through Christ.

Ephesians 1:7–9

If any of you needs wisdom to know what you should do, you should ask God, and he will give it to you. God is generous to everyone and doesn't find fault with them.

James 1:5

However, the wisdom that comes from above is first of all pure. Then it is peaceful, gentle, obedient, filled with mercy and good deeds, impartial, and sincere.

James 3:17

Work

Entrust your efforts to the LORD,
and your plans will succeed.

Proverbs 16:3

Don't work for food that spoils. Instead, work for the food that lasts into eternal life. This is the food the Son of Man will give you. After all, the Father has placed his seal of approval on him.

John 6:27

When people work, their pay is not regarded as a gift but something they have earned. However, when people don't work but believe God, the one who approves ungodly people, their faith is regarded as God's approval.

Romans 4:4–5

God's choice does not depend on a person's desire or effort, but on God's mercy.

Romans 9:16

God in his kindness gave each of us different gifts. If your gift is speaking God's word, make sure what you say agrees with the Christian faith. If your gift is serving, then devote yourself to serving. If it is teaching, devote yourself to teaching. If it is encouraging others, devote yourself to giving encouragement. If it is sharing, be generous. If it is leadership, lead enthusiastically. If it is helping people in need, help them cheerfully.

Romans 12:6–8

There are different spiritual gifts, but the same Spirit gives them. There are different ways of serving, and yet the same Lord is served. There are different types of work to do, but the same God produces every gift in every person.

1 Corinthians 12:4–6

God has made us what we are. He has created us in Christ Jesus to live lives filled with good works that he has prepared for us to do.

Ephesians 2:10

I'm convinced that God, who began this good work in you, will carry it through to completion on the day of Christ Jesus.

Philippians 1:6

My dear friends, you have always obeyed, not only when I was with you but even more now that I'm absent. In the same way continue to work out your salvation with fear and trembling. It is God who produces in you the desires and actions that please him.

Philippians 2:12–13

Slaves, always obey your earthly masters. Don't obey them only while you're being watched, as if you merely wanted to please people. Be sincere in your motives out of respect for your real master. Whatever you do, do it wholeheartedly as though you were working for your real master and not merely for humans. You know that your real master will give you an inheritance as your reward. It is Christ, your real master, whom you are serving.

Colossians 3:22–24

Here is another reason why we never stop thanking God: When you received God's word from us, you realized it wasn't the word of humans. Instead, you accepted it for what it really is—the word of God. This word is at work in you believers.

1 Thessalonians 2:13

Certainly, we work hard and struggle to live a godly life, because we place our confidence in the living God. He is the Savior of all people, especially of those who believe.

1 Timothy 4:10

Therefore, a time of rest and worship exists for God's people. Those who entered his place of rest also rested from their work as God did from his.

Hebrews 4:9–10

We want each of you to prove that you're working hard so that you will remain confident until the end. Then, instead of being lazy, you will imitate those who are receiving the promises through faith and patience.

Hebrews 6:11–12

Worship

I will proclaim the name of the LORD.
Give our God the greatness he deserves!
   He is a rock.
      What he does is perfect.
         All his ways are fair.
He is a faithful God, who does no wrong.
   He is honorable and reliable.

                 Deuteronomy 32:3–4

You alone are the LORD.
You made heaven, the highest heaven, with all its
    armies.
You made the earth and everything on it,
   the seas and everything in them.
You give life to them all, and the armies of heaven
    worship you.

                     Nehemiah 9:6

The LORD is my strength and my shield.
My heart trusted him, so I received help.
My heart is triumphant; I give thanks to him with
   my song.

The LORD is the strength of his people
   and a fortress for the victory of his Messiah.

Psalm 28:7–8

I waited patiently for the LORD.
   He turned to me and heard my cry for help.
   He pulled me out of a horrible pit,
      out of the mud and clay.
   He set my feet on a rock
      and made my steps secure.
   He placed a new song in my mouth,
      a song of praise to our God.
         Many will see this and worship.
         They will trust the LORD.

Psalm 40:1–3

   Why are you discouraged, my soul?
   Why are you so restless?
      Put your hope in God,
         because I will still praise him.
            He is my savior and my God.

Psalm 42:5

Whoever offers thanks as a sacrifice honors me.
I will let everyone who continues in my way
   see the salvation that comes from God.

Psalm 50:23

I want to give thanks to you among the people, O
Lord.
I want to make music to praise you among the
nations
  because your mercy is as high as the heavens.
    Your truth reaches the skies.

Psalm 57:9–10

Let the nations be glad and sing joyfully
  because you judge everyone with justice
    and guide the nations on the earth.

Psalm 67:4

God, the God of Israel, is awe-inspiring in his
  holy place.
He gives strength and power to his people.
  Thanks be to God!

Psalm 68:35

Come, let's worship and bow down.
  Let's kneel in front of the Lord, our maker,
    because he is our God
      and we are the people in his care,
        the flock that he leads.

Psalm 95:6–7

The Lord rules as king.
  Let the earth rejoice.
  Let all the islands be joyful.

Psalm 97:1

Hallelujah!
Give thanks to the LORD because he is good,
  because his mercy endures forever.

Psalm 106:1

With my mouth I will give many thanks to the
    LORD.
I will praise him among many people,
  because he stands beside needy people
    to save them from those who would
      condemn them to death.

Psalm 109:30–31

Praise the LORD, all you nations!
Praise him, all you people of the world!
  His mercy toward us is powerful.
  The LORD's faithfulness endures forever.
Hallelujah!

Psalm 117

Break out into shouts of joy, ruins of Jerusalem.
  The LORD will comfort his people.
    He will reclaim Jerusalem.
  The LORD will show his holy power to all the
    nations.
All the ends of the earth will see the salvation of
  our God.

Isaiah 52:9–10

If you stop trampling on the day of worship
    and doing as you please on my holy day,
if you call the day of worship a delight
    and the LORD's holy day honorable,
if you honor it by not going your own way,
    by not going out when you want, and by not
        talking idly,
then you will find joy in the LORD.
    I will make you ride on the heights of the earth.
    I will feed you with the inheritance of your an-
        cestor Jacob.
    The LORD has spoken.

Isaiah 58:13–14

The Spirit of the Almighty LORD is with me
    because the LORD has anointed me
        to deliver good news to humble people.
He has sent me
    to heal those who are brokenhearted,
    to announce that captives will be set free
        and prisoners will be released.
He has sent me
    to announce the year of the LORD's good will
        and the day of our God's vengeance,
    to comfort all those who grieve.
He has sent me
    to provide for all those who grieve in Zion,
    to give them crowns instead of ashes,
        the oil of joy instead of tears of grief,
            and clothes of praise instead of a spirit
                of weakness.

Isaiah 61:1–3

I will find joy in the Lord.
I will delight in my God.
   He has dressed me in the clothes of salvation.
   He has wrapped me in the robe of
      righteousness
      like a bridegroom with a priest's turban,
      like a bride with her jewels.

                                        Isaiah 61:10

Then I will repay you for the years
   that the mature locusts, the adult locusts,
      the grasshoppers, and the young locusts ate
         your crops.
         (They are the large army that I sent
            against you.)
You will have plenty to eat, and you will be full.
   You will praise the name of the Lord your
      God,
      who has performed miracles for you.
      My people will never be ashamed again.
You will know that I am in Israel.
   I am the Lord your God, and there is no other.
      My people will never be ashamed again.

                                        Joel 2:25–27

Then I will give all people pure lips
   to worship the Lord
      and to serve him with one purpose.

                                        Zephaniah 3:9

Praise the Lord God of Israel!
　He has come to take care of his people
　　and to set them free.
　He has raised up a mighty Savior for us
　　in the family of his servant David.

Luke 1:68–69

Peter answered them, "All of you must turn to God and change the way you think and act, and each of you must be baptized in the name of Jesus Christ so that your sins will be forgiven. Then you will receive the Holy Spirit as a gift. This promise belongs to you and to your children and to everyone who is far away. It belongs to everyone who worships the Lord our God."

Acts 2:38–39

Praise the God and Father of our Lord Jesus Christ! Through Christ, God has blessed us with every spiritual blessing that heaven has to offer.

Ephesians 1:3

You heard and believed the message of truth, the Good News that he has saved you. In him you were sealed with the Holy Spirit whom he promised. This Holy Spirit is the guarantee that we will receive our inheritance. We have this guarantee until we are set free to belong to him. God receives praise and glory for this.

Ephesians 1:13–14

Jesus Christ will fill your lives with everything that God's approval produces. Your lives will then bring glory and praise to God.

Philippians 1:11

Always be joyful in the Lord! I'll say it again: Be joyful! Let everyone know how considerate you are. The Lord is near. Never worry about anything. But in every situation let God know what you need in prayers and requests while giving thanks. Then God's peace, which goes beyond anything we can imagine, will guard your thoughts and emotions through Christ Jesus.

Philippians 4:4–7

You received Christ Jesus the Lord, so continue to live as Christ's people. Sink your roots in him and build on him. Be strengthened by the faith that you were taught, and overflow with thanksgiving.

Colossians 2:6–7

We always have to thank God for you, brothers and sisters. You are loved by the Lord and we thank God that in the beginning he chose you to be saved through a life of spiritual devotion and faith in the truth. With this in mind he called you by the Good News which we told you so that you would obtain the glory of our Lord Jesus Christ.

2 Thessalonians 2:13–14

Therefore, a time of rest and worship exists for God's people. Those who entered his place of rest also rested from their work as God did from his.

Hebrews 4:9–10

The things you do are spectacular and amazing, Lord God Almighty.

The way you do them is fair and true, King of the Nations.

Lord, who won't fear and praise your name?
You are the only holy one,
and all the nations will come to worship you
because they know about your fair
judgments.

Revelation 15:3–4

The angel showed me a river filled with the water of life, as clear as crystal. It was flowing from the throne of God and the lamb. Between the street of the city and the river there was a tree of life visible from both sides. It produced 12 kinds of fruit. Each month had its own fruit. The leaves of the tree will heal the nations. There will no longer be any curse. The throne of God and the lamb will be in the city. His servants will worship him and see his face. His name will be on their foreheads. There will be no more night, and they will not need any light from lamps or the sun because the Lord God will shine on them. They will rule as kings forever and ever.

Revelation 22:1–5

Knowing God's Promises

A Plan of Salvation

God makes promises. He cares enough to take personal interest in what happens in his world. More important, he is wise enough to know what should be pledged, what works for our good and his glory.

Most important, he is able to do all that he says he will do.

As you see in this collection of Bible texts, God's promises extend to every corner of life with encouragement and challenge. Not all the promises of Scripture apply to all people in all times. Some of the promises in this book were specifically directed to individuals or groups. Still, these promises often teach principles of God's concern that apply to us in moments of weakness, doubt, and fear.

A psalm writer who lived centuries before Jesus Christ came to earth, thought about God's promises and what they mean:

O LORD, your mercy reaches to the heavens,
    your faithfulness to the skies.
Your righteousness is like the mountains of God,
    your judgments like the deep ocean.

You save people and animals, O LORD.
Your mercy is so precious, O God,
　　that Adam's descendants take refuge
　　　in the shadow of your wings.
　　They are refreshed with the rich foods in your
　　　house,
　　　　and you make them drink from the river of
　　　　　your pleasure.
Indeed, the fountain of life is with you.
　　In your light we see light.

Psalm 36:5–9

Unfortunately, some of these promises—the light by which we see light—aren't for every person. Many people want good things in their lives, but they don't care to know the giver of those good things. They do not have the relationship that God has said he desires of a people he calls his.

The Bible speaks of God's promises as his acts of love and acceptance of those who love and accept him. He has set aside those who know him to himself and given them lavish guarantees of what he has done, is doing, and will continue to do. Being one of God's people means accepting the one God sent to save us. The well-known promise of John 3:16 is that "God loved the world this way: He gave his only Son so that everyone who believes in him will not die but will have eternal life."

John 1 in the New Testament looks at the coming of Jesus and the promises that were fulfilled in him. John described Jesus as "the Word"—God's greatest communication with humanity—for in Jesus, God himself came to dwell in human form:

> In the beginning the Word already existed. The Word was with God, and the Word was God. He was already with God in the beginning. Everything came into existence through him. Not one thing that exists was made without him. He was the source of life, and that life was the light for humanity. The light shines in the dark, and the dark has never extinguished it.
>
> John 1:1–5

John goes on to declare that we can have a personal relationship with Jesus and, by believing that he is God, become God's children:

> However, he gave the right to become God's children to everyone who believed in him. These people didn't become God's children in a physical way—from a human impulse or from a husband's desire to have a child. They were born from God.
>
> John 1:12–13

Jesus said, "I am the one who brings people back to life, and I am life itself. Those who believe in me will live even if they die. Everyone who lives and believes in me will never die. Do you believe that?" (John 11:25–25).

What must you believe concerning this source of life in order to have it? The Bible's answer is that first you must face the evil that you have done and admit that you cannot be God's unless Jesus takes away your dirtiness and makes you acceptable.

God cannot have evil in his majestic presence, and we all do the things he forbids. The book of Romans tells us, "There is no difference between people. Because all people have sinned, they have fallen short of God's glory" (3:22–23). We fall short of whatever moral standards we set for ourselves, let alone the standards set by a creator who is perfect and holy. Without an answer to sin, none of us can escape the judgment that God has also promised.

Our hopeless plight changed dramatically when Jesus Christ, "God with us," took personal sins vicariously on himself and accepted God's judgment. Jesus fulfilled God's promises by accepting God's rejection and death although he was without sin.

Romans 5:21 makes this promise that explains what happened: "As sin ruled by bringing death, God's kindness would rule by bringing us his approval. This results in our living forever because of Jesus Christ our Lord."

After admitting our need, the second action we must take is to believe that Jesus is the one he said he was and accept him as our ruler, our "Lord." When one man asked how to be saved, he heard the wonderful promise, "Believe in the Lord Jesus, and you and your family will be saved" (Acts 16:30).

There is nothing else that anyone can do to be accepted by God. Jesus said, "I am the way, the truth, and